For the Love of CATS
The *Caring* Guide for Owners

For the Love of CATS

The *Caring* Guide for Owners

by Ingeborg Urcia, Ph.D.

1985

First Edition • First Printing

HOWELL BOOK HOUSE INC.
230 Park Avenue
New York, N.Y. 10169

Library of Congress Cataloging in Publication Data

Urcia, Ingeborg.
  For the love of cats.

  1. Cats. I. Title.
SF447.U75 1985   636.8   84-25189
ISBN 0-87605-812-8

Contents

Part Two
The Breeds

About the Author

INGEBORG URCIA, Ph.D., has been breeding and showing Russian Blue and Cornish Rex cats under her cattery name of Katzenburg since 1971. Besides raising and showing some grand champions and regionally winning cats, her special interest is the study of feline personality and behavior.

Her writing career about cats started when she was asked by a Russian Blue newsletter editor to contribute an article on kitten behavior modification. The article was well received and led to numerous others in cat magazines, international cat periodicals, breed publications and cat association yearbooks. She writes a bi-monthly column for a German cat magazine, and a monthly feature on kittens for the *Almanac,* the official publication of the Cat Fanciers Association (CFA). Her breed book on Russian Blues is the first ever written about that breed, and her book on Rex cats has become the standard work on the American Rex.

Her interest in animals is not limited to cats. She has obedience trained dogs. She is involved in a number of people-pet partnership programs for young people and senior citizens. She has served as a 4-H judge and is editor for the newspaper of SpokAnimal C.A.R.E., the local humane society.

In her non-cat life, Dr. Urcia is a professor at Eastern Washington University in Cheney, Washington. She, her husband and numerous cats, some elderly Huskies and a Schipperke live on a ranch and tree farm near Cheney. Her two children share her interest in animals. Her daughter is studying at veterinary school in Pullman, Washington, and her son, who has just finished law school, has raced Siberian sled dogs.

Introduction

THERE ARE some twenty-three million cat people in the United States. Other people *own* horses, dogs, goldfish, or no pets at all. Cat people live with cats.

A cat person is easy to spot. She is the woman at the supermarket checkout counter with the shopping cart full of cat food cans, and one little box of tissues. He is the man whose knit pants sport little loops at the knees. Cat people get up at five in the morning and drive hundreds of miles through a snow storm to a cat show. Cat people have houseplants that hang from the ceiling. Sometimes they may appear a bit strange, but they know a special secret. They know that a small, furry paw softly touching your cheek when you are sad can make you feel better. They know that a kitten with a ball of string can be more amusing than a famous TV comedian, and, most of all, they know that a small animal weighing less than ten pounds can have a big heart full of love and devotion.

The book is written for cat people, especially those who want to learn more about living with their four-footed friend. Not too long ago, most cats led a simple life in country surroundings. For exercise they played outside in the grass and trees, their diet was supplemented by hunting and foraging, and for entertainment they watched all outdoors. Today, there are still barn cats who make a living down on the farm, but most cats, like most people, live in less rural surroundings. City streets do not make safe playgrounds, and mice are rarely a problem on the 32nd floor of a high-rise apartment building. Today's city or suburban cat leads a sheltered life. This is not really bad. Unlike his country cousin, who lives a short life threatened by disease, stray dogs, and automobiles, our house pet has a chance to enjoy his natural life span in health and safety. He is cherished and cared for, and in turn is able to provide his owner with companionship and love. But the secure life also raises some unique problems. What does a cat do for exercise in the limited space of a city home? And what about a diet for a feline who knows mice only from picture books and the Saturday morning cartoon shows?

This book is intended to answer the questions of the contemporary cat owner. It is not intended as a technical manual. Information about the feline reproductive system can be found in any encyclopedia. The cat owner is more likely to be interested in what happens when his Cinderella comes home after having escaped for a night of revelry with the black tom in apartment 13. Veterinary texts will tell him about strange diseases with long Latin names, but how can he tell whether kitty is ill in the first place? He does not want to know how to arrange living quarters for a 30-cat cattery, but only how to make his home comfortable for his one cat and himself.

Part One

A Cat in Your Life

1

Kittens Are Special

WE HAVE ALL LEARNED in school that nature equips all creatures with complex means of survival in a hostile world. Bears hibernate, birds fly south for the winter, and a cactus stores water in the desert. A kitten may be a very vulnerable creature, but never underestimate the powerful charm he has been given to help him find a new home. If you don't believe this, just try to walk past the window of a pet shop where three or four striped kittens are practicing their antics. Even worse, visit a local cat show with the firm intention of not, *absolutely not,* buying a cat. Steel yourself to ignore a large pair of innocent eyes in a fuzzy little face, don't let yourself be touched by that furry little paw, and close your ears to the ecstatic purr that emerges from a pile of kittens cuddled together for a nap. Chances are that you will be taking one of them home despite your resolves.

Should You Acquire a Kitten?

A kitten is his own best salesman—too good sometimes for his own welfare. Because he is so cute, he is taken home by the parent who lacks the will power to resist the begging of the children for the little "toy" (which scratches when it is mishandled), by the woman who temporarily forgot the no-pet policy in her apartment house, or by the man who was so captivated that he did not remember that his wife sneezes at the mere mention of *cat.* Too soon, reality intrudes and the carelessly bought kitten must go—to the pound, to the animal shelter, or to abandonment in the streets.

The true cat lover knows that he is buying a companion who will be with him for years to come, and he considers carefully what he expects from his new family member. First of all is the question of age. Should he start with a small kitten or a full-grown cat? The kitten has all the charm of a

These Russian Blues will make excellent pets. Kittens raised with love and care become rewarding, lifelong companions. *Matlock*

A playmate helps an active kitten grow into a well-adjusted cat. These Russian Blue brothers are inseparable.

Before selecting a kitten, acquaint yourself with his care and requirements. Longhair kittens like this Maine Coon demand grooming to be happy and well cared for.
Reimann

baby, and is entertaining and playful. But he also shares the naughtiness, helplessness, and need for love and attention of a young child. If you want something small to raise, educate, and watch over, take a kitten, but not one that is younger than ten to twelve weeks, no matter how adorable. Younger kittens may have been weaned too early, they may not have been reliably litter trained as yet, and, worst of all, they may not be properly socialized. Such a kitten may grow up into a neurotic grouch or a timid misfit who is afraid of his own shadow. Unless you have misanthropic tendencies that you want your cat to share, do not select too young an animal.

But what if it drives you to distraction to teach your kitten that swinging from the drapes is not good, clean fun; if you hate to find a small, hard rubber ball in the toe of your shoe; or if you don't relish running back during your lunch hour to serve young tom his cottage cheese? Consider adopting an older cat. Such an animal has already learned that people have strange prejudices when it comes to their furniture and clothing, his stomach hs settled down to one or two meals a day, and he may actually surprise you with his nice manners and well-taught ways. He has acquired a distinct personality, and may have become the refined, quiet lady or gentleman that you desire for a roommate.

Male or Female

The next question to decide is whether to get a male or a female. Here, again, personal preference should be the factor, but you should also know what you are getting. A male of any cat breed is generally more affectionate than a female. This does not mean that Buffy does not love her owner, but she has been conditioned by nature to love her kittens, too, and because of this responsibility she will always be a bit more wary—an essential feature of the protective mother.

The male, on the other hand, is a big, lovable slob who comes unglued when you rub his stomach, and forgets everything in the ecstasy of having his chin scratched. True, when he gets to be eight or nine months old, other interests intrude. There are lady cats to be courted, and cat rivals to be fought, and it is absolutely necessary to have him neutered. An unaltered male does not make a good pet. The female does not have those problems, and many people prefer her for that reason. But she, too, will be entranced some day by the tuneful wooing of a feline suitor, and her yowling, rolling, and carrying on during her heat is no pleasure either. An altered cat of either sex makes an excellent pet.

Finding Your Kitten

With questions of age and sex settled, a new problem emerges. Where does one get a kitten or cat? There are many people who will tell you that such a question is ridiculous. They assure you that they have never bought a kitten, and that their sleek or fluffy cat simply appeared at their door one morning. Such things do happen to the country dweller or the suburbanite, but if you live on the 23rd floor of an uptown apartment house you are not likely to meet a stray. There is the lop-eared, battle-scarred tom that turns over the garbage cans in the alley, or the poor, starved kitten with the matted coat and the weepy eyes. If you wish to help one of them, you must spend a lot of care, both physical and psychological, on such a rescue mission. Perhaps you prefer to go to the humane society and adopt one of their orphans. Perhaps you should call the lady who advertises free kittens in the newspaper. Both places may provide you with a handsome companion or a sick, scared, neglected animal. If you are a Good Samaritan, it may be personally gratifying to help a stray or adopt an orphan.

Then again, you may be one of the people who admire the aristocratic bearing, the well-cared-for beauty of the purebred animal. You dream of the glory and prestige such a handsome pet will give you. Go to a cat breeder. If he is reputable and senses your good intentions, he will try to provide you with a pet of your dreams or direct you to someone who can. Pet shops also advertise purebred cats, although much less often than purebred puppies.

What to Look For

Whether you adopt a kitten from your neighbor's tabby, or buy one from a cattery that advertises purebred Burmese, you must now proceed with caution. "Let the buyer beware" is an old proverb. The cat who will share the next 15 years with you should be healthy, stable, well-mannered, and loving. How can you tell all these qualities? Take a good look. A healthy kitten or cat should be clean, and should come from a clean environment. No matter how fancy the breed, and how many ribbons hang in the breeder's living room, take a close look at the cats' quarters. Has the litter pan been cleaned recently, or do you meet at the door with an overwhelming odor that says *dirty*? Does mama cat interrupt her nap frequently to scratch at her ears or her neck? Ear mites and fleas are unpleasant guests, and can cause health problems such as worms. Do the cats and kittens sneeze in unison? Respiratory illness can spread like wildfire. Do the kittens run and play energetically or do they sit around sadly with tears in their eyes? Weepy eyes are often a symptom of disease. And what about mama cat, is she clean and well cared for? Remember the old saying, "like father like son, like mother like daughter." Healthy parents have healthy offspring. If you have a chance, look at papa, too. Then ask about shots. Every kitten should have his first set of vaccinations at the age of eight or nine weeks. This includes immunization against panleukopenia, rhinotracheitis, and calicivirus. A second booster is given

Kittens are babies and, like small children, need a lot of sleep. *Mhara O' Buachalla*

Each kitten is an individual, as the differences in expression among these Abyssinian litter mates clearly show. *Jim Story*

17

at 12 weeks of age. Some people with other cats also insist that the newcomer be tested for leukemia. Such a test is now available, and while it is not entirely conclusive, it is a protection against spreading this dread disease. Has the kitten been wormed recently? Worms do occur in the best of families, and a bit of prevention can go a long way.

A sickly animal may be a pathetic sight and may appeal to your pity, but you are better off without him. All you will get is a lot of heartache and expense. For the same reason, do not choose the runt of the litter. Such a measly fellow does sometimes surprise everyone by catching up and becoming the giant of his family. More often, however, he will have also been the one who had the least chance at adequate nutrition, and he is more likely to become ill. A clean, shiny coat, bright, alert eyes, a firm body, and energetic movements are the signs of a healthy kitten, and such a one should be your choice.

But stop! Didn't we say earlier that your kitten should be of stable and affectionate temperament? How can you recognize these qualities? The best way is to get acquainted with the little fellow. Sit on the floor and meet him on his own level. To a tiny, three-pound kitten you look like a veritable giant, and he does not know you as well as his own giants. They are harmless, but who knows, you may plan to eat him for lunch. Even older cats find a total stranger somewhat unnerving. So get down on the rug, wait, and observe. Pretty soon, the boldest of the family will return, sniff your foot, and if nothing alarming happens, will start to untie your shoe laces or climb into your lap. Before you know it, the whole bunch will be crawling all over you, except for the cute little soul with the serious eyes who is still watching gravely from the sidelines. Don't be tempted by his cute, grave manner—he is shy and will make an invisible companion. Take the bold fellow instead, the one who came to you right away. He loves people and trusts them, and will make an excellent pet.

If the kitten you are selecting is from a cattery and not from a neighbor's pet, you will also want to know if he was cattery or house raised. A kitten whose first months of life were spent away from human companionship in a small cattery cage, and who has not adjusted to household noises and strange faces, will have a hard time getting used to you and to your home. This one may remain shy and withdrawn all his life. Of course, if the little tortie your neighbor tries to pawn off on you was raised under the front porch, chased by humans and frightened by dogs, she too won't be a satisfactory companion. The best kitten will have had a loving start in life as a family member. He has learned that people are really nice, and such a fellow will be the kind you should take home.

By now you have probably made your choice and selected your new pet. If he is of the "All-American" garden variety, he is ready to go with you and occupy his new home. Ask the breeder for the details of his diet so that he can continue to be fed the same foods in the same manner. An upset

18

An outdoor pen allows growing kittens to safely observe the world. *Mhara O' Buachalla*

He may never fill your shoes, but very soon he will have an important place in your household. *Cox*

Even very young kittens learn quickly about their new home, although this Rex kitten pretending to tell time is definitely a fraud. *Reimann*

If you are looking for one of the more unusual breeds, such as these Cornish Rex kittens, attend a nearby cat show where such kittens may be offered for sale. *Cheney Free Press*

19

stomach is not a good way to start a new life. A favorite toy or blanket may also help to ease your kitten's loneliness during the first few days. No other preparations are necessary.

But perhaps the kitten you selected is a blue-blooded aristocrat. In such a case, the cat breeder will want to know more about your plans. Do you merely want a handsome representative of your favorite breed? Then get a pet-quality kitten. Such a kitten will not fit the standards of his breed closely enough for competition. His ears may be too small or too big, his eyes too yellow or too green or even a bit crossed, but this will not matter since he is never going to compete in a show. Instead, he will be a handsome companion with all the advantages of his breed. And he will cost less. His more expensive brother may be a better show prospect, but he won't be a better pet.

The Show Prospect

Should you desire the glory of the show ring and the admiration that surrounds a true show cat, consider a show *alter*. He will combine the best of two worlds—his name in lights, and his home with you. You will pay a higher price than for his humbler brother, but sometimes a breeder has a cat that needs to be altered for a variety of reasons and is happy to find a good home for him. Such a cat may be an excellent show cat, and you will have a bargain.

And then there is the top show kitten. Let me hasten to add that such a cat is not common. Don't expect every ugly duckling to turn into a swan—most of them stay right in the chicken yard. Most breeders know their cats far too well to let a future Grand Champion slip through their hands. Can you be trusted to spend the time, resources, and effort to show such a kitten in the manner he deserves? (*Campaigning* is the term used in cat show circles.) You may actually have to talk the breeder into letting him go to you. In addition, such a kitten will have to be quite a bit older than the pet candidate, since even the most experienced breeder cannot always assess the potentials of a three- or four-month-old youngster. If you pay the sometimes astronomical price for such a paragon, you can expect rightly to get an animal of top quality, but do not believe the breeder who guarantees absolute show success. Too many variables such as future development, personality, and competition are involved in the creation of a top winner, and absolute success is impossible to predict. An honest breeder will tell you all about outstanding parents and grandparents, and about his hopes that a certain kitten will follow in their footsteps. There is such a thing as beginner's luck, but more likely it is good planning, keen observation, and plain hard work that have gone into the creation of a top show winner.

Now that you have purchased a show kitten, you are entitled to his registration papers, as well as a detailed pedigree listing all his ancestors.

Figure 1
How to Make a Simple Cat Bed

Enlarge the pattern pieces as indicated. Cut two of piece A and one of piece B from a heavy fabric (fake fur is the most elegant but cotton, denim, or corduroy will do). Sew the A pieces together, right sides facing one another, leaving an opening. Turn inside out and stuff with fiber fill (not too full) and stitch the opening closed. With the right sides together, fold the long strip in half so that it is now 27″ × 12″ and sew the long sides together. Stuff tightly with fiber fill and sew it around the perimeter of the circular pillow (C). Overlap the open and closed ends of the long strip and sew closed.

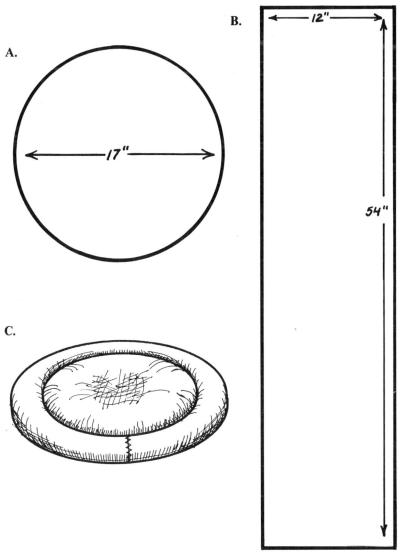

Check to see that only the breeds permitted by one of the registering associations appear there. In the case of the so-called natural breeds, all ancestors must be of the same breed for at least three generations. But if your kitten belongs to a mutated breed like the Rex, or a man-made breed like the Himalayan, certain other breeds have been used for outcrosses. Such crosses are, however, strictly regulated by the registering associations. Also make sure that the association that has registered your kitten is represented in your area. Otherwise you may not be able to show your pride and joy.

Pet-quality purebreds are sometimes sold without papers, or occasionally a breeder will give you papers only after you supply proof that the kitten has been neutered or spayed at the proper age. Discuss such arrangements in detail before you make your purchase to avoid disappointment later. And do not buy a kitten with a provision attached, such as co-ownership, a breeding arrangement, or a future kitten-back guarantee. Such deals may appear attractive since they usually involve a smaller cash outlay, but later the provisions may be hard to fulfill. A simple, clear transfer of ownership is best. Of course, since a purebred is quite expensive, you should demand health and temperament guarantees. An honest breeder will agree to have you take the kitten to your vet for a health checkup, and will take him back if you find, after a few days, that you are not satisfied with his temperament or personality. Try to be considerate, too. No breeder will want a kitten back after six months just because you are no longer interested in him. If necessary, establish such conditions in writing. This will avoid future unhappiness and disagreement.

And so the day has finally come, and the kitten is now yours. As he cuddles into the new, fluffy bed that you have thoughtfully provided for his comfort, you suddenly realize that he has become much more than the sum of all the qualities you have selected so carefully. Purebred or alley raised, he is no longer just "the kitten." He is Tigger or Tabby or Beauty, he is a personality, and he is special—not because all kittens are special, but because he is yours.

2

What Every Well-Mannered Kitten

Should Know

THE LONG-AWAITED DAY has arrived, and your kitten will soon share your home with you. A catnip mouse is ready for tiny paws to bat it around, a soft, fluffy bed is ready for its new occupant, and you have stocked enough cat food to feed a circus of hungry lions.

Welcome Home—Tragedy or Triumph?

In an hour or two you will be able to hold and pet the little creature to your heart's content. Stop! The scene you are picturing in your mind may look quite different. Two scenarios follow.

The kitten has arrived and is slowly emerging from his traveling carrier. The trip has been frightening. There have been strange noises and rude joltings, and he is glad to get out of the cramped box and stretch his legs in peace and quiet. But peace and quiet he does not meet. Instead, he is faced with a sea of strange faces, strange hands that reach for him, loud voices that talk excitedly, and perhaps even Rover, the trusty family dog, who adds to the confusion. Horrors! Kitten decides this is worse than all the travels, and dives for safety under the sofa, the only available shelter. Great disappointment. Everyone has been so anxious to see the little newcomer, and now he is out of reach. Let's get him out! And so he is poked at, prodded, and thus retreats even further behind the furniture. Finally there is quiet. The family has temporarily given up and settled down to dinner. Kitten is thirsty and hungry, too, and decides to risk a peek from under the sofa. Nobody is looking? Good. Carefully he emerges, but he has been seen. Again eager hands reach, loud voices assault his ears. Again he disappears under the sofa, and this time he won't come out until everyone has gone to bed. Days pass, and kitten is still an elusive guest, rarely seen. Finally the family decides he is just too nasty (one of the chases resulted in a scratched finger) and shy, and will have to be sent back, or worse, go to the pound. The sad thing is that all this disappointment is not necessary, and matters could have been handled better.

Let's replay the scene differently.

Kitten has arrived and is slowly emerging from his carrier. The trip has been frightening. There have been strange noises, rude jolts, and he is glad to get out of the cramped box and stretch his legs in peace and quiet. He looks around and finds himself alone in a small room with a clean litter pan and small dishes of food and water set out invitingly. Apparently somebody is glad to see him. But right now he is tired, and after having a snack and a drink and a visit to the litter pan he curls up for a long, welcome rest. A few hours later, refreshed and calm, he is ready for new adventures. Soon the door opens, and he wanders out and around the house. There are strange people, strange voices, but they pay no attention to him. Reassured, he decides to investigate, and rubs against some legs situated conveniently. No reaction. Hey, don't you see me here? Are you blind? And he takes his courage and jumps up on the lap belonging to the legs. Now he is petted and welcomed until he decides to do a bit more exploring, and leaves again. No one tries to restrain him. And after a few days, kitten has forgotten that his home has ever been anywhere else, and has become a full-fledged family member.

Now which of the two scenes do you want to play? If you opt for the second, you may have to restrain your desire to pet your kitten a bit longer, but he will much more quickly become all you want him to be for the rest of his life—a friendly, people-loving, playful companion.

Getting Acquainted

Of course, he is still a very young fellow, and needs to learn a great deal about you, and you about him. First, what are his needs? They are easily met—three square meals a day if he is quite young, a few simple toys, a clean and convenient litter pan, and a soft place to sleep. Soon you will find out what his moods are, when he is ready for a bit of fun, and when he would rather rest or eat.

In the morning he will replace any alarm clock by demanding his breakfast much earlier than you are ready to feed him. Why aren't you up? Can't you see the sun is shining? Don't you hear his stomach growling? He

24

A bright-eyed, alert look is a sign of good health. These two Russian Blues seem to be waiting for something wonderful—probably dinner. *Jal Duncan*

Kitten games are preparation for later hunting skills. This little fellow practices paw/eye coordination. *Atkins*

Catch! This Rex kitten is ready for a game.
Atkins

has a busy day ahead, and must soon take his seat by the window to watch the sparrows' flight in the tree nearby. This is so exciting that his chin trembles, and he makes a funny, chattering sound. Noon means a bit of cottage cheese or egg, and then a long nap on his favorite chair in the afternoon sun. Dinner is the highlight of his day. Anxiously he weaves around your ankles while you prepare his meal. Hurry up, he is starving. One look. What, Kitty Delight again? Guess I'll pass for now. And your "starving" cat turns away in boredom, only to sneak back in a few minutes later in order to clean his dish. Mustn't be too eager. In the evening his favorite spot is on the TV set—nice and warm—where he can dangle his tail into the picture. Suddenly something on the screen attracts his attention. He jumps down and sits close for another look. Hey, what's running there? Little paws grab at the moving cartoon figures. Where did they go? Let's look behind. Naw, too boring. And back up he hops for his nap.

Yes, soon you will be familiar with his needs and his day, and won't be able to imagine your home without him. You won't even mind that soon all your knit clothes have little loops. Get a nail clipper, one of the "people" kind since pet clippers are meant for dogs and are much too big. Gently press his paw until the claws are extended to full length, then carefully snip off the tips. Be sure not to cut into the pink area. This hurts and he will never forgive you. Claws grow as quickly as fingernails, and such clipping sessions should be repeated weekly. Once he is used to them, he won't mind.

Housetraining

But a true friendship depends on a mutual give and take. While you have to consider his needs, he must also conform to yours. Many people feel that cats cannot be trained, but that is not true at all. Let's start with that all-important litter pan. If your kitten came to you at the age of twelve weeks, he should be completely box trained, and know what the litter is for. Most cats are cleanliness fanatics and will be only too eager to dig into a nice box of clean litter. Any brand will do, but avoid the one that has chlorophyll to prevent unpleasant odor. That stuff is irritating to the eyes of many cats. As for the unpleasant odor, a pan that is regularly cleaned and washed out with soap and water does not develop an offensive smell. Never use any cleaning product with phenol—it is very bad for your cat's health. You expect your family kitty to have good toilet manners as a matter of course, but once in a while there is a little fellow who does not get the word. Don't despair, there are remedies. Try to establish the reasons for his aberrant behavior first. Assuming that there is no physical problem, he might be frightened to use the litter pan. Perhaps in order to get there he

26

must pass a frightening object. Sometimes an older cat will not permit the newcomer to use the pan. This is mean, but it does happen. So the kitten, rather than brave the obstacle, selects a safe corner instead. Move the pan and see if that helps.

A second possibility is that your kitten hasn't yet learned what the litter pan is for. Perhaps he was raised on the streets and alleys, and needs some formal education. Here an older pet will be the best teacher. If one is not available, you must take him whenever he has sinned and place him in the pan. Move his legs back and forth, and hope he will get the message. And be sure to wipe the spot of his mistake with some white vinegar to remove the smell, or he will return to use it again. If he seems unusually dense, you may have to confine him until he learns. Place him in a small cage or carrier that is just large enough to admit his bed and a small litter pan. In order not to soil his bed he will use the pan, and soon get the idea. Don't let him out until he shows signs of consistently using the pan, no matter what he promises you. Once he does, he should still not be given the run of the house. Lock him in one room with a pan, or preferably several. Only when he is consistently using the litter tray should he be released to the freedom of his entire home.

A strange situation does arise when a kitten has been trained to use newspapers rather than litter. Many breeders do this since the papers cost so much less, but it is not a practice to be recommended. The papers are smelly and not very absorbent, and a kitten so trained may be tempted to leave his mark on any newspaper that is left carelessly on the floor or a chair. When a paper-trained kitten is left for the first time with a litter-filled pan, he won't know what to do and will probably soil the floor. He, too, should be confined, but in addition to the litter, leave a piece of newspaper in the pan, covering about half the surface. Once the kitten has learned to use the paper in the pan, reduce the size of the paper until eventually you are only putting in a tiny piece as a reminder. By now, your kitten will use the litter, and finally the paper may be removed entirely. But you will always be able to tell such a paper-trained kitten from others of his kind by the fact that he will never bury his droppings like other cats. The paper training has never given him a chance to learn this.

Training and Personality Development

Just as your kitten can be box trained, he can also learn other socially acceptable behaviors. One of the main virtues in a well-taught cat is his gentleness. A tiny kitten must learn to have velvet paws. Every time he plays with you and shows his claws, gently pinch the inside of his paws. As a reflex, the claws are sheathed and he is then praised. Kittens thus trained will never put out their claws when playing. Biting for fun is another

At twelve
weeks of age
a kitten is
ready to take
on the world
and to go
to his new home.
Oswald

This kitten is just a bit young for his first set of
shots, which should be given at the age of
about eight weeks.   *Keyes*

No two kittens are alike. Some are brave,
while others prefer to hide behind a
brother.   *Ashley*

28

objectionable habit. The next time he playfully grabs your finger with his teeth, don't jerk back. Simply stop any movement of your hand but leave your finger in his mouth. Since you really don't taste to his liking, he will immediately stop biting, and after two or three times he won't nibble again. Tell him firmly "No," and praise him in a quiet voice when he stops.

What else would you like him to know? He is a smart fellow and will learn good manners if you are consistent, but don't permit one day what you forbid the next. That is too much for his tiny brain, and he will get confused. If the kitchen counter is a no-no, then it should be a no-no every day, and not only on Mondays and Tuesdays.

Want him to come when you call his name? Just start calling him whenever you are ready to feed him. Soon his name will take on very pleasant associations and will set him running to you. Keep it that way, and don't call him to give him medicine or to lock him up. Once fooled, he won't be so trusting again. Incidentally, if his name is Ebenezer Scrooge, he may have some trouble figuring out who is called by that handle. T. S. Eliot notwithstanding, cats react better to a short, simple name, preferably one with an "i" sound in it. Of course, he could also be trained to come at a whistle or a clicking sound, if those are associated with dinner. If the latter is your signal, you may see a stampede toward the kitchen every time you absentmindedly click your teeth.

Some people who have cats should have chosen a dog instead. True, a kitten can be taught to fetch and carry, to roll over and play dead, or to give voice, but fortunately he has enough independent spirit to perform such tricks only when he feels like it. If this is not your idea of obedience, try a Sheltie or a Poodle. They are marvelous obedience dogs who truly enjoy their work. A cat will never be quite easy—his tricks are more spontaneous, and usually are initiated by him. For the same reason, a cat on leash will never produce the same results as a dog. While Rover or Spot walks mannerly beside your left knee, matching his speed to yours, Kitty surges ahead, winds around your ankles, trips you, and suddenly decides to sit down for a quick wash. This is not to say that cats cannot be taken out on leash. A harness and a leash may be the only means by which your house tiger can enjoy the fresh air and green grass of the back yard. For his safety, he should never be permitted to go out alone. But if you two decide on a trip, don't expect him to heel, and don't take him into the street. You are merely inviting disaster in the shape of a dog, or ridicule when Tommy trips you up. Many cats fight a collar and leash desperately. They need to be accustomed gradually, first to the wearing of a harness, then to the attached leash that is dragged around, and finally to the person who attaches himself to the other end. If they learn to tolerate all three, you have a leash-trained cat. Don't expect any more.

Remember the day when your kitty arrived? Months have passed, and you two are beginning to make a marvelous team. He knows you well, and you have started to know him a little. You have adjusted to his needs and he is learning to conform to some of yours. Once a rough country bumpkin, he is now on his way to becoming a well-mannered, sophisticated family cat. Shake hands on it—your association will be a long and pleasant one.

3

Dogs Are People Too

CATS HAVE a reputation for being rather solitary pets, and if your cat is the sole animal occupant of your home, he probably won't mind this state of affairs, as long as he can get plenty of attention from you. Of course, if your work keeps you away all day, he might get bored and be happier with a companion, another kitten or a puppy. In some instances cats have even learned to make friends with such unlikely companions as a guinea pig, a parrot, or even a mouse. The secret of such compatability lies in the age at which the animals are introduced, and in the matter of introduction.

New Cats—Old Cats

Introducing a new kitten to an older household cat is usually quite easy. Kittens have a charm of their own, and even the crustiest old feline tyrant will tolerate a playful, innocent, fearless bit of fluff. Of course, the old-timer has to establish his rights, and frequently will do so with quite a bit of hissing and even growling. The newcomer learns that it does not pay to be the first at the feeding dish, and that old Pasha does not like to have his tail pulled while he is sleeping. Since most kittens have already experienced this kind of reprimand from mother or litter mates, it does not upset them much. Do not worry or interfere in these getting acquainted rituals unless there are signs that the threatening behavior is turning into actual violence. After a few days, your kitten will have learned where he may not trespass and when not to disturb the ruler of the house, and all will be peaceful again. In fact, a sedate older cat may suddenly discover again that playing ball and chasing a tiny kitten is as much fun as it used to be during his younger days.

An older cat will almost always accept a young kitten. The best age for introducing them is when the kitten is about twelve weeks old. Here a Himalayan and a Cornish Rex share a home.   *Shirley Miller*

The first meeting between a new kitten and the resident cat may be a bit stormy, but these matters should be left for the cats to settle.   *Brockelsby*

Introductions are more difficult when the newcomer is also a grown cat. Here animosities may flare up that may set the scene for lifelong dislikes. For one thing, most cats are very sensitive to smells, and the new pet's smell may be offensive to the established cat. Sometimes it helps to rub both animals with a cloth soaked in vinegar. This eliminates the differences in smells, and both now smell the same. In general, however, it is best not to confront the two cats with each other on the first day. Give tempers a time to cool down, and let the newcomer feel more secure. If possible, let him spend the first night in your home in a room by himself. Your old pet knows, of course, that he is in there and may try to peek or sniff under the door. Let his curiosity build up, and let him get used to the idea of another animal gradually. When the new cat does appear, his presence is no longer quite the unexpected shock. Another very effective way of introducing older cats to each other is practiced in larger catteries. If you have a collapsible wire cage (a cat carrier will do also), place it in the middle of the room with the new cat inside. This gives both pets ample time to inspect and sniff each other without actually being able to do much fighting. Soon the novelty will have worn off, and the old cat may forget that the newcomer hasn't been there before. Then it is time to open the cage door and let him join the crowd.

I have referred to the new cat as "he" merely for the sake of consistency, but one thing must be clearly understood. It is possible to introduce two females to each other in a fairly peaceful manner, also a female and a neutered male, or even two neutered males if they are still young enough, but two unaltered males will always fight, and in many cases an unaltered tom won't even tolerate a neutered colleague.

Cat Meets Dog

If the original pet is a dog rather than a cat, introductions have to be handled a little differently. First, it is necessary to find out how your dog feels about cats. Some dogs love those little furry things, and contrary to popular legend, cats and dogs are not born mortal enemies. But there are those dogs who react to the sight of a harmless kitty like the proverbial bull to the red cloth. Such cat-haters are made, not born, and often their master is partly responsible for this attitude. What fun it is to chase a cat down the street, especially if one is encouraged by one's owner saying, "Get the kitty." What fun—until kitty has had enough and turns the tables. Rover gets his nose scratched, and henceforth feels rather unkindly toward the entire species. Yet even such a dog may end up chasing stray cats from the yard while his own cat watches and seems to applaud.

Since the dog, in most cases, is the larger animal, make sure that any meeting for the first several days takes place under close supervision with the cat on a safe perch from where he can survey the situation. Of course,

Dogs and cats can and will be friends if properly introduced. Here a Manchester Terrier and a Russian Blue share a nap. *Standing*

If your cat is an only pet he will not be unhappy, but will be pleased to rule the household and bask in your undivided attention.

occasionally the problem is reversed. I know a Chihuahua who is deathly afraid of cats, and whose domestic life is made miserable by a large, aggressive tom with whom he is forced to share his home. Once you have established that both animals are basically friendly toward each other, they can be trusted alone together, and may eventually decide to be friends for life, sharing board, bed, and play. If the dog is very large, he may sometimes be a bit rough with his friend, and the owner should make sure that he does not unintentionally injure the cat. It is usually better if the two animals are fairly close in size.

Strange Bedfellows

And what about the strange friendships between unlikely animals that sometimes make newspaper captions? Usually such animals have either been raised together, or a mother cat decides to adopt a tiny orphan of another species along with her own babies. Attempts to foster such friendships because the owner considers them cute often end in tragedy, and are only successful if the animals take the initiative. Remember, the little dog who befriends a lion in the zoo, and whose picture appears in the evening paper, may well be only one in a series of dogs, since the lion's devotion frequently proves fatal to his current friend. The same may be true for the cat and the rat sharing a pillow. When the game gets rough, the tiny pal may well become the victim of too realistic play.

Cats and Children

Sometimes a new arrival of a different kind puts a strain on the relationship between pet and master. What happens when a new baby joins the family? Cats have a nasty reputation of sucking away an infant's breath or smothering a baby in his crib. Such horror stories are, of course, unfounded, and most babies are probably safer around a cat than a dog, whose possible jealousy may cause him to bite and actually harm the child. Cats are usually quite curious about the new little creature that makes funny sounds. Rather than leaving the first encounter up to chance, take your cat and introduce him or her to the baby, and watch what happens. Once they have seen the new family member, cats generally take the situation in stride. They seem to realize that the child is something like a kitten, and when the baby begins to crawl, it is often the patient cat who permits him to maul her in a way that she would never tolerate from an adult. If matters get too annoying, she will merely walk away. A young kitten, of course, does not understand, and will react to rough treatment by unsheathing his claws. It is better not to bring a very young kitten into the house where there is a toddler, until the child is old enough to be taught gentleness for the little creature.

This little boy and his Devon Rex kitten will be long time friends. _Crocker_

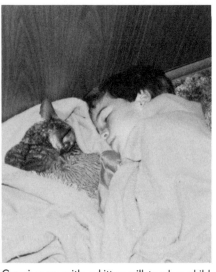

Growing up with a kitten will teach a child love and understanding for animals. _Manus_

Kittens and children can be a wonderful combination if the child is taught how to handle his pet. _Manus_

A cat, unlike a dog, will only accept you on his own terms, but will be a devoted friend who is happy to share most of your activities. _Manus_

One of the things a child should be taught is how to pick up a cat. Never lift him by the scruff of the neck. This is what mother cats do, but they have little other choice. A kitten or cat should be lifted by placing your hand under the stomach and supporting the length of the body with your arm. Always use two hands and do not let the legs dangle. Many cats feel very insecure when picked up with only one hand. And although some cats love to be turned on their back, others object strenuously, and in their effort to turn right side up may scratch you.

A Cat in the Family

When you introduce a new kitten or cat to the family, it often turns out that one member becomes the favorite of the cat. This may be very annoying to the actual owner (or rather the person who thought he was the actual owner). If the cat has been a present for a particular family member and attaches himself to another, much disappointment may result. Again, proper introductions may ease the situation. Never restrain the cat against his will if you want him to come to you. Instead, let him make the first move. If he sidles up to you, don't reach for him but pretend he is not there. This, of course, is intolerable to him, and he will jump into your lap. You may now pet him, but keep your hands off and don't hold him down. Otherwise he will run away. If he is allowed to leave when he chooses, he will be back. A bit of food may help to cement the friendship, but it is surprising how few cats let themselves be bribed with tidbits. Personal relationships are apparently more important to cats than dinner. A cat owner told me about her tom, who regularly used to disappear every Thursday night. Wondering where he spent that evening, she followed and saw him perched at a neighbor's window where he watched a weekly card party with great interest. Since no food was offered, or even eaten, the cat was obviously interested in those human actions that must have seemed amusing to him.

So, if you kitty is lonely, get him a friend. And if the friend is canine rather than feline you can observe the two "living like dogs and cats," that is, living peacefully together.

4

Your Home Is My Jungle

MANY PEOPLE BELIEVE that there is a tiger in every cat, but kittens know from the moment they take their first wobbly steps that they were born to be monkeys. To achieve this goal, they practice endlessly swinging from branches, climbing tree trunks, and descending gracefully from steep cliffs. Unfortunately for your little cat, however, the average home boasts neither palm trees nor tropical vines nor steep mountains. No problem, says your junior Tarzan, as he scoots up your new drapes, balances daringly across the curtain rods (look Ma, no hands!), and does swan dives onto the sofa. He does not understand that the results of this exuberance are seen in tattered fabric and scratched surfaces, and even if he did, he would not care. Scolding him is of little use. At best, he will refrain from playing his games in front of you, and will go into another room to enjoy himself. After all, he has no other outlet for his energy, and your house or apartment is really his jungle. But before you resign yourself to living with rags and wrecks, take heart. There are two possible recourses to dampen his wild spirit until he has reached a more mature and sedate age. They are prevention and punishment.

Toys and Games

Prevention is the better of the two. Recognizing that your kitten really needs an outlet for his natural instincts of climbing and running, you have to provide him with chances to do so. There are numerous items on the market that can help him exercise, ranging from a jungle gym for cats consisting of several small ladders that are joined together, to a little box with a toy mouse attached by a rubber band. Every time the mouse is pulled out from its hole, the rubber band snaps it back in. There are also cat

This lucky cat has a safe outdoor exercise pen. But if your family cat stays inside only, he will be just as happy. *Elisabeth Weber*

A fireplace is a favorite meeting place for indoor cats, as this Abyssinian trio has discovered. *Jim Story*

hammocks, punching bags, swings, and what not, as a look at the ads in any cat magazine will show. They all have one thing in common: they cost money. Fortunately for you, your cat has simple tastes, and while he will enjoy sophisticated cat furniture, he will also appreciate homemade equipment. One of the greatest cat exercisers consists of several empty cardboard boxes stacked at different angles. Your cat will spend happy, active times, jumping in and out, stalking an imaginary foe, and finally falling asleep inside. Equally fascinating for kittens and cats is a grocery bag, which offers chances to crawl in, tip over, jump out, and grab you unexpectedly. To make your cat jump, attach a piece of rope somewhere near the ceiling, but make sure it is too short to touch the floor. If you set it in motion, your kitten will try to catch the swinging end, and will perform some high jumps of truly Olympic quality.

Your cat's favorite game will be one in which you participate. A string dragged around the house, or twirled in a circle will give the most energetic kitten all the exercise he needs trying to catch up with that elusive rope end. Some cats are avid broom chasers, but that game can turn into an annoyance for the owner and should not be encouraged.

For solitary amusement, there are toy mice made of rubber, little hard balls, bones, and other objects that can be purchased in any supermarket or variety store. Generally, these seem to be more suitable for dogs than for cats (even if the manufacturer assures you otherwise) because puppies are much more mouth-oriented and will have fun just chewing on the rubber while cats, unless they are teething, would rather fetch, carry, and attack. Most of these toys are too big and hard for a cat to manage, except for a very small foam rubber ball that a kitten can grab with his teeth. However, such a ball should not be small enough to be swallowed accidentally. More popular are soft items such as fabric mice or small fabric balls. These can be bought, or you can easily make them yourself from some scraps. Commercial ones are often stuffed with catnip but this may turn out to be more of a disadvantage than an inducement. Young kittens are not interested in catnip at all, and some older cats never acquire the taste. Those who do, on the other hand, get really carried away and will do anything to open up the toy to get at the catnip. They roll around and slobber all over it, and all that is left after a while is a very unattractive piece of wet rag. Cotton stuffing is better, and the toy will last quite a bit longer. Just make sure, if you make it yourself, that the stitches are very tight, and that there are no small, loose parts that can be torn off and swallowed.

Household items often make the most successful and inexpensive toys. A piece of paper crumpled into a ball can give a lot of enjoyment to your cat, and the crinkly noise it makes adds excitement. Two pipe cleaners twisted together are also very popular, and my cats have always preferred them to anything else. Some cats see possibilities for games in everything that surrounds them, and carry off pencils, erasers, and small household

40

Figure 2
How to Make Simple Cat Toys

Cat Rattle. Remove the top and the bottom from a small, empty fruit juice can. Wrap and glue a piece of shiny foil or bright fabric around the can, letting about half a can's length of material extend beyond the can on both ends. Tie one end of the covering with a piece of string. Put a few pebbles inside the can, and tie the other end of the covering up. Your cat will love to roll the rattle along the floor or you can attach a longer string to one end and drag it around for her.

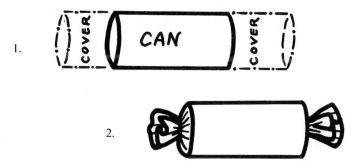

Fabric Mouse. Enlarge pattern pieces A and B. Cut two pieces of pattern A and one of pattern B out of heavy cotton or felt. Cut slits as indicated in both A pieces. Leaving an opening, sew the A pieces together, right sides of the fabric facing each other. Turn inside out. Pull piece B through the slits in the head so that the round ends extend on both sides to represent ears. Stuff with fiber fill and sew the opening closed. Sew a string to the rear for a tail. If you like, you can embroider eyes and a nose.

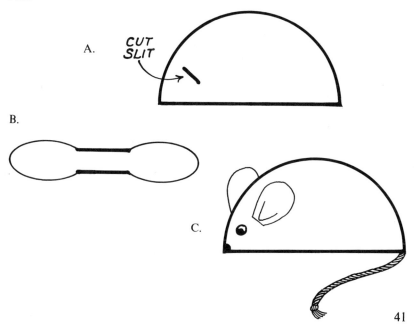

41

Indoor life has its compensations. *La Vond Thompson*

A Russian Blue, a Maine Coon, and a Cornish Rex share the view from a sunny apartment window. *Reimann*

items with great enthusiasm. Old socks make great objects to fetch and carry, but don't leave your other socks around when you play this game. Cats cannot tell the difference, and you may think some very unkind thoughts early some morning when you grope behind the washing machine or the refrigerator to retrieve your new socks, which your cat has thoughtfully deposited there.

The Scratching Post

Of course, amusing your cat is only one purpose of these games. The other, more important, is to prevent destruction of your furniture and rugs by an overly energetic or bored cat. A scratching post is the most important piece of equipment in keeping your cat a civilized companion. Again, you can go all out and purchase a floor-to-ceiling model with numerous platforms and cubby holes, and your cat will love it. These contraptions are quite expensive, but many cat owners have told me that the post is well worth the price since it helps to save their more expensive furniture from the damage done by cat claws. If you are moderately skilled with a hammer and nails, you can build a scratching post yourself. An acceptable one does not have to be several feet high, it only needs to be long enough to allow your cat to stretch out full length against it. A piece of wood mounted upright or at an angle makes an excellent post as long as it is sturdy and does not tip over. No cat will ever again go near a scratching post that tipped, and made it appear ridiculous and clumsy. The success of the post also depends quite a bit on the texture of its fabric covering. Cats love a tightly woven material, somewhat coarse in texture, and with prominent threads running vertically. You might also consider these preferences the next time you shop for an upholstery fabric for your easy chair, and select something less attractive to your feline companion.

By the way, your cat isn't really *sharpening* his claws on your best velvet chair. Each claw has a thin, transparent covering that grows and needs to be sloughed off frequently. The scratching helps to get rid of it. Clipping off the tips of the claws sometimes helps your cat, and reduced the need to scratch. It also prevents snagging when your cat walks across sofas and chairs.

If the scratching post has been constructed to the satisfaction of your cat, only occasional reminders should be needed to keep him from wrecking your other possessions. But once in a while, a cat is so stubborn, stupid, or merely forgetful that even the most glamorous scratching post will not stop him from clawing the upholstery. In such cases, and only if every other means has failed, you might consider declawing. This is a very controversial operation, and opinions vary greatly about it. Some authorities feel that declawing has little adverse effects if it is done to young kittens, but most are strongly opposed. A cat that goes outside must, of

This kitten
plays king
of the hill
on his cat tree.
La Vond Thompson

A cat tree
offers many
possibilities
for exercise
and play and
also saves
wear and tear
on the furniture.
La Vond Thompson

Cats love
to crawl into
small spaces
like this
cat house.
Goforth

course, never be deprived of his basic weapons of defense, but even an inside cat may feel very threatened without claws, and may turn into a neurotic biter. This is why most breeders are opposed to the practice, and why cats without claws are not admitted to cat shows.

Falls

Cats love high places, and a window sill is a fine spot to supervise what is going on in the world. Make sure that such supervision is only done behind closed windows. Contrary to popular belief, cats and kittens do not always survive a fall from a high place, although they do have an amazing ability to twist around in the air and land on their feet. Young kittens have not yet learned to do this, and are especially vulnerable since they often miss their footing and are naturally clumsy. I have seen a kitten fall from a sofa and sprain his tail even though the fall was from less than a foot high.

When Punishment Is Needed

Jungle gyms, kitty hammocks, and other toys and gadgets are fun, but they will not altogether prevent your kitten from doing things he is not supposed to. This is where effective punishment comes in. Needless to say, punishment that does not catch up with the culprit, and that is not administered at the scene and time of the crime, is useless. Your cat knows nothing funnier than to watch you jump angrily up and down while he perches on the curtain rod out of your reach. By the time you have dragged a chair to the spot and started to climb, he is long gone. Or you can almost see the smirk on his face as he works his claws up and down the back of a chair while you frantically search for something to swat him with. In order to make an impression on your cat, the punishment for crimes has to be immediate, far reaching, and unexpected, and the answer is a water pistol or plant mister. The first time your cat is caught in the act, and is hit by a cold stream of water from way across the room, his belief in your superior powers is promptly restored. No matter how far away or how high up he is, you are able to get him. A few well chosen applications of cold water accompanied by a loud, stern "No" should reform even the most hardened sinner. How often you will have to repeat this process depends on how stubborn your cat is, but in the end the discomfort from the unexpected bath will cure him of his misbehavior. If he has been scratching on furniture, shoot him with water, then pick him up and place him on his scratching post and work his feet back and forth. That should refresh his memory. A word of warning, however: Never consider shooting your cat or kitten with a water pistol as a joke. It should only be done as a deterrent. Otherwise the effectiveness is lost, and your cat will consider you mean and cruel.

A little catnip or grass will give your cat a taste of the outdoors. *Goforth*

Watching the outdoors through a window is entertaining for a cat, and does not necessarily mean he wants to go out. *Janet Morris*

Cats and Plants

To your kitten, your home is not only furnished with climbing equipment, but like a true jungle it often boasts some greenery and foliage. Let's face it, cats and house plants are a rather incompatible combination. Either the cat mangles the plants, or the plants may poison the cat. What do you do when you love your bird's-nest fern almost as much as your birdbrained Abyssinian? One solution is to hang the plants in pots from the ceiling where they can be admired but not touched by furry paws. Another possibility is to specialize only in plants that are not attractive to cats. From personal observation I have learned that a small citrus tree is not very tempting to a cat—apparently the leaves taste too lemony. Other small trees such as a weeping fig also do not offer much to interest a kitten. A palm tree, on the other hand, is almost irresistible with its waving fronds, and so is a Norfolk pine if it is small enough to break easily. Boston ferns and Christmas cacti are gourmet items which cats love to chew, and which they will eventually destroy by doing so. Even thorny cacti seem to be attractive to some cats who then manage to get stickers in their tongue and need a trip to the vet to be treated.

Poisonous Plants

As destructive as cats can be to houseplants, the danger of poisoning your pet by letting him eat certain types of greenery is even worse. The following popular plants are very bad for your little friend:

Hyacinth, Daffodil—the bulbs cause nausea and vomiting when ingested

Oleander—the leaves are extremely poisonous for animals and humans and can cause death

Poinsettia—the leaves are fatal—one leaf can kill a cat or a child

Diffenbachia (Dumbcane)—all parts cause burning of the mouth and can lead to death if the tongue swells and blocks the air passage

Castor Bean—the seeds are extremely poisonous, and a single one can cause death

Mistletoe—the berries can be fatal for humans as well as cats

In addition to these house plants, your cat should not have access to the following outdoor plants, which are also quite harmful:

Larksonia—young plants or seeds can cause digestive upsets and depression and can be fatal

Autumn Crocus—the bulbs cause vomiting and nervous excitement

Lily-of-the-Valley—the leaves and flowers can cause irregular heartbeat, digestive upset, and disorientation

Iris—the underground tubers cause severe digestive upsets

Foxglove (Digitalis)—the leaves can cause dangerously irregular heartbeat and digestive upset

Bleeding Heart—the foliage and roots can be poisonous in large quantities

Rhubarb—the leaves, either raw or cooked, can cause coma and death

Daphne—the berries are extremely poisonous

Laurel, Azaleas, Rhododendron—quite poisonous in all parts

Jessamine—the berries cause digestive disturbances and can be fatal

Yew—the foliage is very toxic, and death is sudden and without any warning signs

Several other plants, such as the philodendron, have proven fatal to cats although they are not toxic to humans. Always check whether the plant you are planning to acquire is safe for your cat, or put it out of reach. True, outdoor cats live their entire life around poisonous plants and never dream of chewing on them, but they also have a wide variety of other greenery, especially certain grasses, to nibble. Nor do they have to sit day after day near a particularly tempting plant. To cut down on the temptation such plants may offer your indoor cat, offer him a small pot planted with grass just for him. He will appreciate it, and may leave your palm tree alone.

Other Household Hazards

House cats certainly have the advantage over their jungle cousins in that they live safe lives, away from the dangers that lurk outside. But is your cat's "jungle" really that safe? Unless you are very careful, your cat faces many deadly hazards in his home environment. Foremost, perhaps, is the danger of being trapped. Cats love to squeeze into small, tight places where they can hide for a nap. Generally this is no problem since they do not become stuck, but what if such a tight place is inside a washing machine or the warm dryer? Never turn on either of these appliances without making sure where your cat is. The same caution should also be applied to a dishwasher. Cats have learned to open the door and look for leftovers on plates. The inside of a folding sofa or daybed may sound like an unlikely place for a kitten to get trapped, but I know of a case where a kitten was folded into one and suffocated. Another dangerous spot is the hot burner on top of your kitchen stove. A cat who suddenly jumps on top of the stove may scorch his soles on the still hot coils of the electric element, and it is a good idea to cover a burner with a pot lid until it has sufficiently cooled after being turned off.

A hazard that can be fatal but is most likely to happen to young kittens is electrocution as a result of chewed wires. Small kittens whose teeth are coming in will chew on anything, and should not be left alone with

As a safety precaution, hang plants from the ceiling and out of your cat's reach. *Meyers*

Indoor life can offer a world of excitement for your cat. How did this fellow get down there? *Atkins*

Cats and house plants can be disastrous to each other. Be sure your plants do not include any varieties that can poison your cat. *Goforth*

All cats love high places, but this Russian Blue kitten seems to be worrying about getting down safely. *Barrington*

Cats love those fiber-filled beds, which can easily be made at home. *Henneke*

This commercially available litter box has a built-in deodorizer.
"Boodabox," Booda Products

an appliance that is plugged into a wall socket. A piece of aluminum foil wrapped around the cord is an excellent deterrent, too.

Whether your house cat leads a happy life in his home "jungle" is up to you. He will do his share by willingly adapting to your rules, and both of you can look forward to a long and happy relationship.

5

I Want to Be Finicky

Like That Cat on TV

FOR HUNDREDS OF YEARS cats have made their living catching and eating mice, and many people still believe that that is what these feline companions are supposed to do. But, let's face it—your family tiger has probably never even seen a mouse, let alone tasted one. He is the beneficiary of the products of a complex industry that specializes in cat food. "Cats are finicky," cajoles a red tom cat on the television screen. He advises cat owners to buy a certain brand of cat food to please the sophisticated palates of their four-legged friends. Other commercials show cats dancing and breaking into song for the sheer joy of a bowl of crunchies, or even ordering their favorite variety over the phone. No wonder the average cat owner asks himself with some confusion which of the many types and brands he should buy. What if his cat does not eat it after a mouthful or two? Remember, cats are finicky! And how should he decide between canned food, moist food, and dry food, each extolled by its manufacturer?

Nutritional Requirements

Perhaps if your cat could talk he would remind you of a few facts about his needs that should be considered first. Like the dog, the cat is a carnivore (that is, a meat eater), but unlike the dog a cat needs about two to three times as much protein. Any sensible diet for a cat should therefore start with a high protein food. Yet a cat food that contains the highest amount of protein is not necessarily the best for your cat. Those brands that declare that they contain nothing but pure meat will, if fed over a prolonged

52

time, cause deficiency diseases. In the wild, the cat lives by catching rodents and other small animals. Beside the meat of the prey, this diet includes grain and vegetable matter from the stomach content, fat, bones for calcium and trace elements, and bulk. In short, a mouse is a complete meal. But since canned mice and birds are not yet available on the grocery shelf, the cat owner has to learn to read the labels on the cat foods to determine how they will meet the cat's needs. Any quality cat food lists the main ingredients as well as a guaranteed analysis of the content. The latter is important since it gives the percentages of crude protein, crude fat, crude fiber, ash content, and moisture.

Ash

Ash content is measuring the remaining matter after the food has been burned. You may have heard of cat food having high ash content, and have been warned against it. The reason for this is that the formation of crystals in the cat's bladder and urine—a condition known as cystitis and very dangerous, especially to the male cat—may be attributed at least in part to a diet high in ash content. The concerned owner will therefore compare food labels and select a brand that is low in ash content.

Moisture

The amount of moisture listed on the can is another figure of interest for the buyer. Translated, moisture simply means the water used in the processing. There is nothing harmful about it, but you may think twice about buying a food with very high moisture content since you are paying for something that comes more cheaply from your faucet. Any food with a moisture content above 75% is too expensive.

Fat

Fat is a nutritional requirement of your cat, and you should not make the mistake of looking at your overweight tabby and deciding he needs to cut down on fat. He may have to cut down on his overall food intake, but a low fat diet is not the answer. Thus a cat food that is high in protein and fat, and low in ash content with no more than 75% moisture is a good basis for your cat's dinner. The remainder of the canned food consists of fillers such as cracked corn, soybean meal, barley, etc. These your cat also requires. Sure, he would enjoy an all meat diet, but it wouldn't be good for him. As to flavors, try to offer a variety. Cats do get hooked on one special flavor, and this may create problems as well as lead to a rather one-sided diet.

Kinds of Cat Food

Some canned foods have enticing names purposely conceived to make

We, too,
are on TV,
but we are
not finicky.

This little Siamese
emphatically demands
his dinner. A healthy
kitten loves his three or
four meals a day.
La Vond Thompson

Alyosha, a Russian Blue, inspects some of the many varieties of cat food available. To find the most nutritious ones for your cat, study the labels carefully. *Urcia*

your mouth water, but remember, your cat can't read. A plain but honest chicken or liver flavor is just as tasty to him, easier on your pocketbook, and usually contains what it says. On the other hand, who knows what is hidden behind such names as Dairy Supper or Feline Delight.

But what about dry cat food? Many people prefer it since it is less messy than canned food, does not smell, and does not need to be refrigerated once it is opened. Dry foods also come in a wide variety of flavors and most cats enjoy their crunchies. To a house cat who has been raised on a soft canned diet, those little hard pieces of dried food are often the only thing that require chewing, and as such are a must in a cat's diet. They serve as a toothbrush, and help rid the teeth of tartar buildup. But they should never constitute the entire diet. If you read the list of ingredients on such a bag of food, you will notice the high ash content as compared to other forms of cat food. In addition, because of the problem of spoilage, dry food is usually quite low in fat content. A diet of nothing but dry food may lead to kidney problems and is not recommended for your cat.

The semi-moist food is often advertised as canned food without a can. What keeps it fresh, however, is an unusually high percentage of sugar, which acts as a preservative agent. Your cat may have a sweet tooth, but sugar is not on the list of ingredients for a healthful diet. If you have ever had a weight problem yourself you know that sugar is a culprit and one of the first items that has to go. Nature has not programmed your cat for it, and it may also lead to making him fat. And who needs a fat cat?

Natural Proteins

Your house cat has certainly come a long way from the hunter of small prey to the supermarket gourmet who thinks that food comes only in those little round cans, and whose dinner bell is the sound of the electric can opener. No wonder that the sight of your hamburger or dinner steak makes his mouth water. Should he have a taste? The answer is yes, in fact you may want to enrich his canned diet and add to the protein content by mixing in some raw hamburger, kidney, heart, or liver. Most serious cat breeders feed a diet consisting both of canned and dry food and raw meat, and since their cats have to be at their physical prime, this practice speaks for itself. Now is the time to strike up a friendship with your neighborhood butcher, since kidneys and heart are sometimes in short supply and only available at certain times. If a bonanza of such meats suddenly appears, you might consider freezing it in feed-sized portions for later use.

Other valuable protein foods for your cat are cooked and boned chicken and boned fish. The latter will probably bring your tiger running from the farthest end of his home, but cats who get too much of it can actually become addicted and refuse to eat anything else. Therefore, unless you are willing to go out every morning for a day's catch of fish to please your feline friend, let him know it is only an occasional treat.

Dairy Foods

Cottage cheese is often recommended for cats because of its high calcium content. It is rich in valuable nutrients and easily available. But most older cats will turn their noses up at it, and those cat authorities who recommend it so highly usually forget to tell you this fact of life. One reason for the low esteem of cottage cheese is that many cats were raised on it when they were small kittens, and who likes baby food once you've grown up? The little kitten who until now has only known milk is usually thrilled with the new taste sensation. He will gobble it up eagerly, until some day he discovers a new treat—meat! After this, cottage cheese becomes something one shakes a hind leg at because it is simply too unmentionable. It is eaten only when there is nothing else. So if your cat is still unspoiled enough to eat cottage cheese, all the better. If not, offer some yellow cheese instead. Some cats prefer the more exotic taste of yogurt, and if neither of these dairy foods appeals, give him a strict look and tell him—never mind, who needs it anyway!

And then there is milk. The fact that cats drink milk is almost as universally believed as the one about mice, and it does not fit every cat either. The kitten that has been drinking cow's milk from the time he was weaned will digest it without trouble. But many cats never develop the enzyme necessary for digesting it and get stomach trouble and diarrhea from the white stuff. So you may not want to offer any. It is not really needed. As for the skimmed or 2% milk that humans drink, no self-respecting cat would even give it a lick. Clean, fresh water fills all the needs and should always be available.

A Complete Diet

A well balanced diet for your little tiger may look somewhat like the following:

Morning: a few pieces of dry cat food, with emphasis on the word "few"

Noon: (for kittens only since older cats need to eat only once or twice a day) cottage cheese

Night: a good brand of canned food mixed with ground raw or cooked meat, and a little dry food

If you want to improve further on it, or if your cat has special problems, you may consider adding some additional ingredients that cat breeders, through trial and error, have found to work for their cats. But

This cat is willing to go to the market for you, but left to his own choices, a cat does not always eat what is best for him.
Ashley

Rex love to eat, and are also eager to help with the dinner preparations. Since they don't always know when to stop, their amount of food should be regulated. *Manus*

remember, each cat is different. The young, growing kitten has a greater need for calcium and protein than the sedentary tabby that spends the day snoozing on your bed. And a slender, active cat burns up his calories more quickly than a heavy, slow moving colleague. Cats living in the dry warmth of an electrically heated apartment may need more oil to keep them from shedding, etc. So choose carefully which of these breeders' tricks will work for you.

Tomato juice—most cats enjoy it, and it adds vitamin C to the food. It is also supposed to prevent kidney trouble because of its high acid content. A small amount can be mixed once or twice a week into the food.

Parsley water—made by boiling fresh parsley, and mixing the resulting liquid into the food. Some breeders swear by this as an antidote for kidney stones. It may not help but neither does it hurt.

Bacon fat—excellent for giving your cat a shiny coat. Most cats love it and make pigs of themselves, so dole it out in small amounts to keep them from overeating and getting sick.

Butter—also good for the coat, but generally too expensive for cat feeding.

Brewer's yeast—manufactured commercially for pets, this adds certain vitamins, and is supposed to be an excellent deterrent for fleas. Apparently fleas do not enjoy the taste of the blood of a cat eating yeast. Anything is possible, and fleas can be a real problem, so you might give it a try.

Wheat germ oil—an excellent source of vitamin E which is especially important for breeding animals. Mixed into the diet once a week, it also supplies the necessary fatty acids for a shiny, healthy coat.

Molasses (unsulphured)—another remedy for excessive shedding. I doubt that your cat will go wild over the taste.

Vitamin and mineral preparations—many of these are on the market. Since most quality brands of canned food already contain vitamins and minerals, these may not be needed by the average cat. Whether you want to add them depends on the quality of the diet you feed as well as on the condition of your cat. Your veterinarian might advise you.

Baby foods—easy to digest for convalescent or poorly nourished animals, also for young kittens. Since baby food does not add to the bulk of the cat, some breeders feed it during cat shows where trim body tone is required of a cat.

Finally, there are a few items that should never be fed to a cat. One is red tuna, which will destroy the vitamin E in a cat's body, causing a painful disease known as steatitis. To be on the safe side, since most people cannot distinguish red tuna in cans from other kinds, it is a good idea not to feed any cat food containing tuna. You will incur the wrath of your kitty friend but avoid possible serious problems. Some people also feel that they are doing their cat a favor by offering chicken bones or by adding a raw egg to the food. Chicken bones can splinter and cause internal injuries, and raw egg white also has an adverse effect on cats. If you want to share your breakfast egg with your cat, scramble it for him unless he prefers it hardboiled or over-easy. Needless to say, your cat should never eat any raw or half-cooked pork any more than you should, and for the same reasons—trichinosis.

The Finicky Eater

So now you have settled on a sensible diet for your cat, and are proud to do the right thing for him. You present him with the appetizing dish you have concocted, but instead of breaking out into a two-step like the cats on TV always do, he sniffs the dish, turns his back, and, adding insults, makes a few scratching motions with his hindleg around it as if to say: "This stuff belongs into my litter box." Are the advertisers right then? Are cats really finicky by nature? Before you throw out the carton of newly purchased cat food and run down to the delicatessen for some caviar, stop and think for a minute. Perhaps it is you, and not your cat, who is really to blame for his finicky behavior. Remember the first days when you got him as a kitten? Didn't he have an excellent appetite, wolfing down everything for fear of having to share it with his no-longer-present brothers and sisters? But then a day came when he was not too hungry and left half of his dinner on his plate. Perhaps he had a slight stomach upset, perhaps he had overeaten the day before. But you, misunderstanding him, decided the poor little fellow did not like Kitty Delight any more, and offered him a dish of leftover chicken livers instead. Wow! What a choice! And so the following day, instead of enjoying Kitty Delight, he was looking for more chicken livers and other goodies—and probably got them. And you got the makings for a finicky cat. If you had left him to his own resources, that Kitty Delight would have looked mighty good the following day, but now he won't touch the stuff. And when the novelty has worn off, neither will he enjoy liver. It may be kidneys next, then truffles—and caviar, here we come. If a cat does not eat his dinner on a certain day, the dish should be removed after a reasonable time. The following day, feed as usual, and chances are your cat will be back on schedule, but give no treats in between.

There is another way to create a finicky eater. All you need is to set down a big dish of dry crunchies. All day long your cat will nibble and nibble, and by dinner time he will be full. Would you be hungry if you had been eating peanuts all day long? A cat who has dry food set out for him all

Who said dinner? A cat pretends to be finicky only if his overanxious owner has catered to his every whim.   *Chappell*

A well-mannered cat should be taught to eat at mealtime and not to nibble all day.
Goforth

day won't only get fat but will also have no appetite left for his dinner. He will merely pick at it, and you have another finicky eater.

So the next time you hear that cat on TV say that cats are finicky, turn the channel and say: "My cat isn't."

The Overeager Eater

The finicky eater has his counterpart in the overeager eater. Some cats, especially Rex, believe that the world was created to be eaten. They gobble down everything that does not eat them first, and at top speed. As a result, they may get sick, throwing up after every meal. Should another cat have the misfortune of sharing their dinner table, he will find his food disappearing before he has even had a chance to find out what smelled so good. A cat who makes a pig of himself in such a way needs to be slowed down. The answer is a deep dish into which the food has been pressed down firmly. This will slow down your greedy eater enough to keep him from getting sick, and will give his fellow eaters a chance to finish theirs before he does. Sometimes, an overeager eater may also profit from being fed in a room by himself, and if he doesn't, at least the other cats do.

Controlling Amounts

Should a cat be allowed to eat all he wants? Some cat authorities will tell you yes, claiming that a cat knows instinctively when he has had enough. These good people have apparently never seen a fat cat. There may be a few hardy souls among the feline population with enough sense and will power to say "enough," but most house cats that spend their life lazing away on sofas—whose only exercise is clawing at your favorite chair—are much too fat and consume more calories than benefits their life style. Their food intake should be controlled, and if this means an occasional dieting spree, so be it. Your veterinarian can tell you if your cat is overweight in case you haven't noticed yourself, and can advise you as to the appropriate caloric intake. An exception to this are young, growing kittens who should always be allowed to eat as much as they want. They will exercise it off, and because of their rapid growth, will need extra nourishment. But once they have reached the age of seven or eight months, supper time should mean enough but not too much.

6

The Patter of Little Feet

YOUR KITTEN has been with you for several months, and you have learned a lot. You no longer worry every time he turns his nose up at the canned hash that the manufacturer has assured you will send him into ecstasy. You have hardened yourself against a pair of innocent eyes, and can bear the icy disapproval in those eyes when you explain, "No dear, the curtains are not meant for swinging." You know that a plaintive little *miaow* in the morning means "I haven't eaten for hours" while the funny *row-row* indicates that you are expected to get the little red ball out from behind the dishwasher for the tenth time. In other words, you think you know your kitty well.

That First Season

But then comes the day when, on returning home, you are greeted by a cat who throws herself ecstatically at your feet and rolls enthusiastically on her back. "All that excitement for little old me?" you ask, and are secretly flattered. But despite all that carrying on, she does not seem to be able to settle down as usual on your lap. Instead, she prowls restlessly from window to door, rubs against your legs, and stops suddenly in the middle of the room, emitting a strange hoarse cry as if in pain. Her rear end raises up as she twists on the floor. Alarmed and sure that she must be suffering, you pick her up and rush her to the vet. And are you surprised to hear that your kitty isn't sick—she is in love!

Yes, the signs of estrus or heat in a female cat can be rather alarming to anyone not familiar with them. But, you say, she is merely a kitten of barely six months. That is plenty old enough, especially if she belongs to one of the more precocious shorthair breeds and has been born in late summer.

Longhaired cats usually mature later, and kittens born in spring seem to grow up more slowly than those that become teenagers during the spring "season of love."

Now that you have been assured that nothing is wrong with Lolita, you begin to wonder what to do with this young sex maniac, who is rolling on your rug and disturbing your sleep with her mournful howling. How long is this supposed to go on? How often will it happen? To both questions the answer is not reassuring if you love peace and quiet. A heat period may last anywhere from a few days to two weeks, and the next one may follow within a week, until your cat has been bred, or until most of the summer and fall have passed. Cats rarely are in season during the winter months. This is usually not a pleasant prospect, especially if your cat belongs to one of the louder-voiced breeds who has to tell the whole world the wonders of young love. So the next question is obvious—do you really want this silly scene to continue?

Spaying

Unless you have serious ambitions as a breeder, the best solution is to spay the female. This will stop all the inconvenience once and for all. Surprisingly, many people are hesitant to take this step. They have heard all sorts of old wives' tales about the problems created by spaying a pet. Since few aspects of pet ownership and care are so full of misinformation and superstitions as the controversy about neutering and spaying, let's look at some of the most common objections.

The most prevalent is usually that a spayed cat will become fat and lazy. This is simply not true. Any cat who becomes fat eats too much and has too little exercise. Unfortunately, this is often the fate of both felines and humans. Perhaps you will consider putting her on a diet. Spayed or not, this is guaranteed to make her weight problem disappear. As far as laziness is concerned, what cat would not be lazy if she had no other interests in life except the next meal? A bored cat is a lazy cat, so add a little bit of excitement to her life. A brisk game of fetch the ball or chase the string may do you both some good, and who knows, your own exercise program may gain new impetus.

But won't spaying change a cat's personality? Yes, it will and fortunately so, because now she will no longer be distracted by such trifles as tomcats, kittens, and sex. Instead, she can now devote all her affection and energy to you. She will be happy to stay home and share your life exclusively.

Of course, you may miss the patter of little feet, and some people will assure you that having a bunch of kittens around is a lot of fun. To those, my advice is to acquire some grandchildren, or to adopt a nephew or niece, or to visit a neighbor with a mother cat and kittens. In other words, enjoy

It is not true that a neutered or spayed cat loses its trim lines and gets fat, unless it is overfed. This Russian Blue spay has kept her figure. Cats are wonderful mothers, but they cannot provide homes for their babies. Too many unwanted kittens are destroyed annually, and neutering or spaying is a humane way to relieve this problem.

Mhara O'Buachalla

youngsters who are someone else's problems. True, it is a lot of fun to watch the antics of kittens, but less fun if those antics involve your spotted geraniums or your damask drapes. Multiply these little mischief makers by three, four, or five and you will have more "fun" than you bargained for. You see, unlike the visiting children or neighbor kittens, these little fellows of your own do not go home in the evening after an hour of play. They stay around and grow, and grow, and grow, and soon the patter of little feet sounds like a herd of elephants passing. Then comes the day when you have to find homes for them, and often the only option is the shelter. Much as you may want to, you can't keep them all since it costs money to feed, vaccinate, and care for a box full of half-grown cats. How much better to have just a nice, well-behaved companion spay instead of a horde of little savages.

Still hesitant because spaying your cat may pose a health risk for her? Have a talk with your veterinarian about it. An operation like that does pose some risks, as any kind of surgery does, but so does the process of birth. In most cases your spayed cat will be up and around within 24 hours.

Neutering

So far, we have only talked about the ladies. What if your kitten is a tom? Then neutering is even more of a necessity. Otherwise you will enter your home one day and sniff suspiciously. What is this terrible lingering smell? It is just old lover boy marking his territory against male competition. If you have never smelled a spraying tom, you haven't missed a thing. If you have, you appreciate the necessity of neutering male cats. So Mr. Tom will have his appointment with the vet, and since his is really a small operation, he will be home again soon, and back to his old, loving self. To avoid spraying incidents, don't let him have a taste of male glory at all, and have him neutered at the age of eight to nine months before he starts to spray. Some people recommend neutering at a younger age, but it is better to give your boy a chance to be fully mature, a process that may not happen if he is neutered too young. Very few males exhibit any "macho" behavior before the age of eight or nine months.

There is one rather serious objection to the neutering of a male, and that is the fear of having him develop urinary problems and the dreaded kidney blockage. Unfortunately, this is a risk that all male cats share. Females block too, but because of their different anatomy it is seldom as serious as in a male. Studies have shown that there is little difference between whole and neutered males when it comes to this disease: it can happen to either one and the exact causes aren't yet known. The only reason why neuters are expected to have a higher percentage of urinary blockage cases is that usually the neutered cat is an indoor cat who is carefully watched. Many a free-roaming, unaltered tom has succumbed to this illness, which can strike within hours and lead to death. His owners simply never learned his fate. Catteries who keep a number of whole males for breeding purposes report the same incidence of kidney problems among their whole cats as among any alters.

Still some reservations? Perhaps you are the proud owner of a pedigreed male cat, and do not want to deprive the feline world of his stud services—which might bring in a nice fee to boot. *Let me disillusion you.* The world will not beat a path to your door. Most cat breeders have their own studs, and if they look for males outside their cattery, they will go to a few top-ranking, all-American males of their breed who have made an exceptional name for themselves in the show ring. Don't succumb to the temptation of breeding your tom once before you alter him—once he's had a taste of the life of a male he may not as easily be reconciled to the life of a neuter. And are you really willing to put up with hysterical females, yowling males, and the entire fuss and bother that goes with breeding cats? You see, it is customary to bring the female to the male, so the whole responsibility will rest with you—the owner of the male. What if a visiting lady suddenly decides to go out of heat. Can you put her up for some weeks until she stops being a shy lily? If you have answered "no" to any of this—hie your boy to the vet. You and he will have a better relationship afterwards, and you can always get a new kitten for him as company.

Do you want to show your cat, and wonder if neutering will ruin his chances? Fear not. The cat fancy, more foresighted than the dog fancy, has always admitted the altered cat for show competition. However, alters compete in their own classes for the reason that otherwise they would have too much of an unfair advantage over their unaltered colleagues. A male or female going through the stress of heat cycles, mating, or kittening rarely has the luxurious coat and stable temperament of an altered cat whose sole aim in life is to be pretty. Alters have no undue distraction. If the truth were known, the real show cat is the alter.

Breeding

In all this, we have assumed that you are the average cat owner who keeps a family tiger for companionship. If you are a serious cat breeder, what are you doing with this book anyway? But sometimes your sneaky Cinderella fools you despite all precautions and slips out the door when your back is turned. You may not even know about her rendezvous with the handsome black and white prince who has been keeping vigil under your window. And now she is pregnant. Too late do you wish that you had made an appointment for her at the spay clinic. Already her increasing girth shows that kittens are on the way.

The first sign of pregnancy appears at about 21 days after the mating.

Six kittens are quite a handful for a Russian Blue mother, since average litters range from three to five. *Ashley*

A proud—
and a little
anxious—
mother watches
her babies.
Mhara O'Buachalla

Siamese kittens are born pure white and acquire the dark mask and points when they are a little older. *Ehle*

67

Suddenly, kitty's nipples are bright pink and slightly enlarged. Two or three weeks later she begins to show signs of getting larger around the middle. You may as well decide to make the best of the situation and learn what will be expected. If the idea of being a midwife scares you, don't worry. Most cats are excellent mothers who instinctively know what to do when the time comes. Even the most inexperienced tabby will know vastly more than you will ever learn about birth and kittens.

For the next few weeks, nothing will happen. Your cat will continue her usual routine, and there is no reason to worry. Feed her a well-balanced diet rich in calcium, and start rounding up prospective parents for the expected offspring. Mama will take care of the rest.

Approximately nine weeks after the first signs of pregnancy, or 63 to 65 days after the actual mating, the cat will be ready to give birth. She will expect you to set up proper quarters for her, unless you prefer to leave this choice to her. She will not mind, but you may if she chooses your linen closet or your bed as the proper place to have her family. A cardboard box lined with newspapers is usually preferable. Set it up in a dark and quiet place, and, if possible, confine her to it during the last few days. If she approves, she will start ripping up the newspapers in her box to make a nest. It will give her something to do since she is obviously not up to knitting little garments. Newspapers are preferable to cloth or towels since kittens can easily get tangled and suffocate in these materials.

The Birth of Kittens

The fateful day has finally arrived. A few hours ago, your cat has been restless, but now she has gone into her box. Sit with her if you can since young mothers are often nervous. A cat with a close relationship with her owner usually prefers to have him around at this time, although some independent souls tell him to get lost. Take your cue from her in this matter. For a while, she is going to be the star of this show. Kittens will arrive after pronounced labor, sometimes within quick succession, sometimes as much as an hour apart. There is little you must do unless the cat is in obvious distress for hours without any kitten being born. In such a case, your vet should be notified. Usually, however, mama cat manages extremely well, and will soon have some wet little bundles of fur contentedly nursing. Each kitten is born in a transparent sack, which the mother tears open with her tongue. Sometimes, if kittens follow each other too closely, the mother will get tired or confused and leave one to his fate. In such a case, tear the sack carefully with your fingers, and pinch the umbilical cord before cutting it with a pair of blunt, sterilized scissors. It is also a good idea to check if all the afterbirths have been expelled, a retained one may lead to infection. Some cats eat this afterbirth, and that is not harmful. The whole birth process may take as little as an hour or last for many hours depending on

Kittens who grow up together will remain great friends, like these two Russian Blues.

Keyes

This litter of kittens is ready to go to a new home, and hopes that you have provided loving families. As breeder, you have a responsibility for their lives.

Ashley

Well-fed, healthy kittens have firm bodies and bright eyes.
La Vond Thompson

Very young kittens have large heads in proportion to their small bodies and feet. They learn to move around very quickly and need to be confined in a safe box during the first few weeks.

Matlock

70

the number and spacing of the kittens, but finally they will all have arrived. You will know because now the mother is relaxed, stretched out on her side, and purring her heart out proudly over her new family.

For the next two weeks, the kittens will spend all their time nursing, and mother won't leave them alone for long. She will appreciate room service for the first few days, and will always hurry back worriedly at the insistent squeaking of her brood. Some kittens are real tyrants even at such an early age and won't let mama stretch her legs without squalling nastily, while others are content to crawl closer to the warmth of a brother and sister. The younger and less experienced the mother is, the more she will worry. An old, experienced cat sometimes seems to say to her kittens, "Shut up and don't carry on like that." And surprisingly enough, that is what they will do.

Many experts will advise you to leave mother and her kittens alone until the litter is older, but that would be a mistake. Now is the time to socialize them if you want them to be people lovers later on. Have you ever noticed the initial reaction of a tiny, blind kitten when someone approaches? He hisses! Instinctively he reacts like his wild ancestors would have. You must win his trust and overcome this reaction. Asking mama's permission, pick him up for a minute with both hands and gently stroke his back. Then put him back and do the same to brother and sister. You will find that in a week or two the hissing will have disappeared. But kittens who have been left to themselves still hiss at the approaching "danger." Of course, these early contacts should be kept very brief so as not to tire out the tiny fellows. Mother will see to that.

By the way, are the kittens male or female? An interesting question, and one that is not easy to answer. Most cat books and veterinarians will assure you that identification is simple. Male cats are supposed to have two dots—a colon—under their tail and females show an exclamation point. Well, none of my kittens were ever punctuated correctly! In fact, I am almost certain that they plot: "So she thinks we are boys. Ha, let's surprise her and turn into girls today." I used to blush at such stupid misjudging of the sexes, which seemed to confirm my ignorance. Then one day my vet confidently pronounced a kitten to be a male, and this same "Sam" later turned out to be "Samantha." After that, I held up my head with more reassurance. Your best bet in sexing kittens is to compare—if you have two and they are not alike, obviously you have one of each sex. Small kittens resemble each other and are often hard to tell apart, so knowing that you have a male and a female, you can wait for another month when the sexing is much more obvious. If you have two of the same kind, you will have to gamble, but again, time will soon reveal the truth. Wait until they are six to eight weeks old, then you can return to the punctuation game—and now you will be able to see the difference. If you are lucky enough to get a tortoiseshell or bluecream, the odds change tremendously in your favor, as torties and bluecreams are almost always females.

The Growing Kittens

Soon those early weeks will pass, and your kittens will have opened their eyes (any time from five to 21 days). Almost overnight, they will grow from little mouselike creatures that only mother can love to fluffy, cute, active miniature cats who are ready to explore the world. Assure them at all times that you are their friend. A kitten is never too young to be petted, played with gently, and held and assured that he is welcome. Quickly, they will get ready to experience the world as adults. At the age of five weeks most are ready to try adult food and will start to wean themselves. If they don't, mother will surely help. Weaning is generally no problem—sooner or later a kitten will stumble into mother's food dish, start cleaning himself, and discover that this sitcky mess feels good on the tongue. There is more where this came from, so back to the dish it is. Before long, all will eagerly lap up soft foods, and you must make sure that mother still gets her fair share before the kittens devour it all. As soon as the kittens are on solid food, potty training begins. Until then, their mother has washed their little bottoms. Now they are on their own. Make sure that at this critical time they are closely confined within easy reach of their litter pan. Otherwise they may decide to use a convenient corner of the room, and once a habit is established, it is hard to break. Toilet training is mainly learned through accident. Again, the enterprising kittens literally stumble into the pan, sniff around, and soon discover what it is for, according to the principle of monkey see, monkey do.

And here are the kittens again, twelve weeks old and ready to go out into the world. They should have had their shots at eight and twelve weeks of age. Don't be tempted to let them go earlier—tiny kittens need their mother, and too early separation will result in sickly or neurotic babies. But if they are old enough,weaned, potty trained, and protected by their shots, they are a family you can be proud of. Hopefully, you have done your share, and good homes are waiting for all of them. This may not be easy, but they are truly your responsibility. Make sure they don't add to the army of unwanted cats who are annually destroyed or who lead miserable lives as scavengers and strays. They deserve better. And while we are on the subject—this time be sure your Cinderella has had her operation before she meets her next Prince Charming.

7

In Sickness and in Health

EVERY VETERINARIAN is probably sick and tired of the old joke that he is lucky because his patient cannot complain about his mistakes. This "advantage" is compensated by the fact that his patients cannot tell him where it hurts either, as every cat owner can testify who has ever tried to find out what is wrong with kitty. Indeed, if you are inclined toward pessimism, your cat can drive you to distraction every time he sneezes or sniffs disdainfully at his food. Is he sick? How sick? Or is he just bored and tired?

Signs of Illness

There are a few time-honored tests that, unfortunately, are not at all reliable. Many people believe that if a cat's nose is hot and dry he has a fever, but the truth is that even cats with cool, wet noses may be sick while one with a hot nose may just have curled up in front of the heater. Ears seem to be slightly more accurate thermometers of a cat's body temperature, but they, too, can be deceiving. The easiest way, of course, should be to check the temperature with a fever thermometer, keeping in mind that the cat's normal temperature is around 101 degrees Fahrenheit. But few cats will tolerate such crude invasion of their privacy, and unless you are really skilled, you will either wreck the thermometer or hurt the cat, let alone get scratched. In any case, since the fever may only be a symptom of a disease, knowing that your cat is running a mild temperature will tell you little.

A much more reliable test is his appetite. Although some cats will skip a meal occasionally because they just aren't hungry or the "mess" isn't worth bothering with, I would be alarmed if my cat would refuse consistently even the most tempting food for two days in a row. Not that there is danger of his dying from starvation, but his lack of appetite tells you he is not feeling well. But be sure he really doesn't eat, and has not just been secretly snacking from your garbage can. A cat that does not drink any liquid is also in danger of dehydration, but here the problem is that most cats rarely are seen drinking, and it is often hard to tell whether he refuses all liquid or is only taking sips when you are not looking. However, dehydration is easily spotted by pulling up the skin on his neck with two fingers. Normally, if you release the skin it should slip back into position quickly. If a dent is left that fills only gradually, dehydration may be present as a result of a health problem. Also, deeply sunken eyes are another warning sign that your cat isn't getting enough or is losing too much liquid.

The best indicator of a cat's state of health is, of course, his overall behavior. For this you must know him and observe. If he is usually energetic and active, and all of a sudden begins to mope around and hide under the furniture, he may be trying to tell you that he is not feeling well. But a large, placid cat whose idea of exercise is to move from the sofa to the chair, will show no unusual behavior by sleeping all day long. So the rule is that any behavior that is out of the ordinary should be carefully observed and checked.

One of the exceptions to this rule happens when your female cat goes in heat for the first time. Rolling and twisting on the floor, screaming, and losing her appetite are not indicators that something is wrong, but to the novice cat owner who has not witnessed them before, they may seem very alarming.

If your cat suddenly fails to clean himself, if he is listless, if he sneezes or vomits, it is time for a visit to the veterinarian. Hopefully, this is not the first time you have given the doctor a thought. Otherwise you may find yourself on a Saturday evening or a holiday (cats always seem to pick impossible times to get sick) calling every animal clinic in the yellow pages for someone to take pity on your poor cat. The first visit to the vet should have come long before, preferably when you first acquired your cat. Let your vet see him when he is healthy, ask for the necessary shots, and have him checked for worms. Then, when a true emergency occurs, the doctor will already be familiar with your animal and you will have established a relationship of trust and confidence.

About Veterinarians

Choosing a veterinarian is, of course, a personal decision, but there are a few do's and don'ts to consider. Do check for cleanliness. This does not mean that the facilities should be lavish. Remember, as you enter the tastefully and impressively decorated waiting room, that someone has to

Bright eyes and a shiny coat are signs of good health. A concerned owner learns quickly to detect signs of illness in his pet. *Mhara O'Buachalla*

A plush, well-groomed coat shows that a cat is feeling well. Sick cats neglect their appearance. *Mhara O'Buachalla*

pay the rent for these elegant quarters and it may well be you. A simple, clean waiting room is all that your cat and you will need. Beware also of the doctor whose receptionist can't schedule your appointment until months from now. This indicates how much in demand he is. Will he take you in even if your cat does not always get sick during office hours? Will he be available for emergencies? How does he feel about crawling out of bed at two in the morning to perform a Caesarean on a mixed breed that only her owner loves? It takes more than a good doctor for this—it takes an animal nut!

Some veterinarians unfortunately display an unwarranted snobbishness. They are perfectly willing to treat your purebred Persian or your high-prized Poodle, but turn up their noses at pets of humbler origins. This is a bad attitude. A good vet should never make any distinctions based on his patient's pedigree or social status.

And how is his bedside manner? My favorite vet greets you with a "How is Brutus today, Mrs. . . . eh?" Yes, he forgets your name but he remembers his patient and that is what really counts. Watch his relationship with the animal, too. It is foolish for a vet to take risks and get bitten or scratched, but one who is unduly tearful isn't going to be very effective either. After all, this is a relationship that is going to endure, and once your domestic tiger has found how much fun it is to scare the vet, you will have a hard time.

Administering Medication

But let's return to our sick kitty. Hopefully, his illness was minor and the vet merely prescribed a few pills, with the order to call back in a day or two if there is no improvement. He tells you that he thinks all will be well. All will be well? Don't believe it, because there are still those pills. Before your unbelieving eyes he measures a few red golf balls into a bottle with the admonition to give them to the cat every three hours. In answer to your worried question on how to get them into your cat, he waves his hand airily and tells you: "Just shove them down his throat or mix them into his food."

Since you trust his scientific authority, you don't ask if there is possibly a liquid or a smaller pill he might prescribe, but pack up your cat and your pills and head home. Soon the fateful hour approaches, and you discover that your cat will have absolutely nothing to do with the medicine. "Over *your* dead body," he says, and means it. So you try one of the three proven methods of pilling your cat. They vary according to the experience and age of the patient.

First, there is the surprise method. You open the unsuspecting cat's mouth and quickly slide a pill into it as far back as possible. Be sure it is centered on the tongue, otherwise he will work it out at the sides. Then hold his mouth open, and he will swallow. Don't hold his mouth shut because that will only aid him in working the pill out at the sides or the front. This method is easier said than done. Unfortunately, it rarely works more than once. An experienced cat can prevent it by simply jerking his head before you have a chance to get the pill back far enough.

Thus, we advance to strategy number two. Wrap your pill-experienced cat in a large towel to keep his feet and claws from digging into you, then give him his pill wrapped in cream cheese. Greedy cats will love the cheese and forget about the pill until it is too late. Smarter ones will try to spit it out, but the cheese will make the pill stick to the roof of his mouth, and he won't be able to eject it until you have closed his mouth. In this method, you hold the mouth shut and wait. It is a contest between your patience and that of your cat, who is waiting for you to let go so he can spit out the pill. If you outwait him, you will eventually see his throat working. He has swallowed. But double check. He may be just fooling you by pretending, and as soon as you let go he will run away to deposit the pill, which he has stashed in a pocket in his cheek.

The third method calls for smashing the pill and hiding it in food. It works generally if the pill does not have a strong, unpleasant taste. I have known clever old cats who carefully unwrap every bit of food they get to check that nothing is hidden in the middle. The other trouble is that a cat whose appetite is poor because of his illness may not want to eat his food, pill or no pill.

If all fails, there is only brute force left. Some people recommend a zippered bag for the cat with an opening only for his head. The combined efforts of two people and the helplessness of the cat in his bag may help you succeed, but often at the price of a bitten finger. So, if possible, ask your vet to give you the medication in liquid form. Compared to administering pills, giving liquids is child's play. Use a small syringe and inject the liquid at the side of the cat's mouth and toward the back. Be sure to push the liquid in slowly to prevent choking. A little may dribble out again, but most will go down his throat.

Some cats develop a nasty trick when giving medicine. They start foaming at the mouth. This is generally harmless but can be quite upsetting to the owner who thinks the cat is going into a fit.

Giving medication isn't exactly easy, but what about the cat who has needed stitches. "Be sure he doesn't pull them out," admonishes your vet. As soon as you get home, your dear kitty starts unravelling. What can you do? Depending on the location of the stitches, a so-called Elizabethan Collar may be the answer. This is a large circle of cardboard or plastic that fastens around your cat's neck and keeps his mouth from reaching any other parts of his body (see Figure 3). Your vet may be able to lend you such a collar, or you can easily make one yourself.

And then comes the day when your sick kitty shows his first real

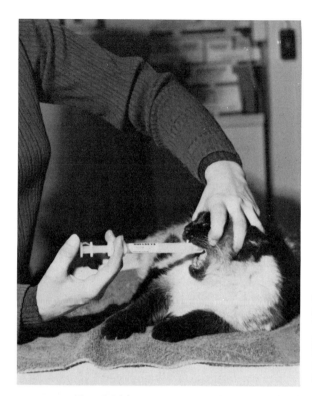

Giving a cat a pill
can be a chore.
This pill gun
prevents bitten
fingers.
*Professional
Specialties, Inc.*

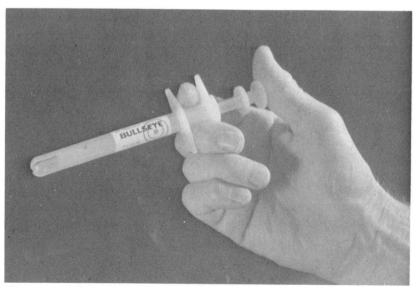

This commercially available pill gun is very handy in medicating a sick cat.
"Dr. Hansen's Bullseye Pillgun,"
Professional Specialties, Inc.

Figure 3
How to Make an Elizabeth Collar

Cut a circle from lightweight cardboard (a cereal box works well). The diameter should be just a bit longer than the measurement from the cat's neck to the tip of its nose. Make a cut to the center of the circle and cut out a round opening a little larger than the cat's neck. Slip the collar around the cat's neck and staple or securely tape the edges together. A reasonably smart cat will have it off in about twelve hours, but it can always be put back again. This will be effective enough to keep the cat from licking or biting at a wound.

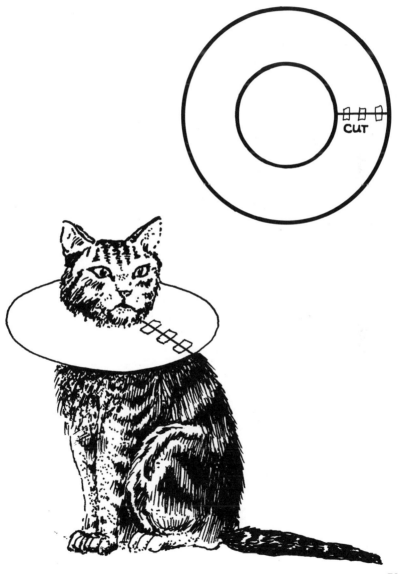

interest in food again. You know he is getting better. Try to tempt him with a lamb kidney—few cats can resist such a treat. If he is supposed to have a lot of liquid, lightly salt all his food. Soon he will be his old self again, and all is well—at least until you get the doctor bill!

Immunizations

A chapter about the sick cat should not end until ways are discussed to keep your cat from getting ill in the first place. True, there is little you can do to keep your cat from catching an occasional "flu bug" or upset tummy, but you can keep him from getting more seriously sick. You can have him immunized. Fortunately for us, science has found a reliable prevention to some of the killer diseases that only ten or 15 years ago wiped out the lives of many kittens and cats. Today, every kitten can be safely vaccinated against feline distemper, also known as panleukopenia. This disease is quite different from canine distemper, but no less fatal. A kitten should have his immunization approximately eight weeks after he has become fully weaned. Otherwise his mother's antibodies which are passed on through the milk, will counteract the development of immunity.

At the age of eight or nine weeks, he should also be immunized against rhinotracheitis and calicivirus (with a booster at 12 weeks). These two, which often appear together, are not always fatal but may cause lifelong side effects. Rhinotracheitis is an upper respiratory disease that causes your cat to sneeze and develop cold symptoms. If not treated properly, your cat may get a chronic respiratory infection that will seriously debilitate him. The calicivirus is responsible for watery eyes and an ulcerated tongue, and may result in permanently blocked tearducts, which can lead to serious eye infections. One of my kittens came down with a relatively mild eye infection before the vaccine was available and developed a virus infection in his eye that led to blindness. This vaccine has one added advantage. It can be given both as an injectable, or as a drop directly on the nose and into the eyes. Discuss with your veterinarian which method he recommends.

While this vaccine has been a life saver for kittens and cats, it should never be given to pregnant cats, nor do I recommend it if you are planning to breed your cat shortly after. Many breeders have found that a cat who has been vaccinated a short time before will not conceive for a while.

Keep a record of these vaccinations, since yearly booster shots are recommended.

And let's hope that your cat will lead a long, healthy, and trouble-free life. But if anything should upset him, at least you will know what do do "until the doctor comes."

8

The Happy Wanderer

CATS ARE HOME BODIES, but there comes a time when even the most retiring tabby will have to face the fact that her owner likes to travel, and she better like it too or accept more unpleasant alternatives such as staying home alone or being packed off to a boarding kennel.

Actually, traveling with a cat is often easier than with a dog, and need not be a problem at all. A cat is small, can be placed into a handy travel case, does not require to be taken out for walks on a leash, and requires a small amount of food, which comes in handy little cans. With a few basic preparations, you and your cat may actually enjoy a trip together. These preparations vary, of course, with the mode of travel.

Air Travel

The most common method of traveling with a pet involves either the family automobile or an airplane. Neither trains nor buses allow pets at this time. Let's talk about air travel first. It has several distinct advantages, and some very serious drawbacks for your pet. First, the good sides. Many airlines now permit a pet owner to bring his animal right into the cabin with him, provided he carries it in a small container that fits under the seat. The airlines will even provide such a carrier at a reasonable fee. Now anyone who has ever traveled on a modern plane knows that space is at a premium, and that there really isn't much room under the seat. But cats do fit into rather tight containers, and you can always offer a reassuring word to your kitty, and tell him that the trip won't be much longer. Be sure, if you plan to take your cat with you on the plane, to make reservations in advance for him, since no more than one pet at a time may travel in the cabin.

For cat owners with more than one pet, and for cats traveling alone, there is air freight. The animal will travel in the cargo room of the plane, in a sturdy container that can be purchased from the airline. Before you commit your pet to this mode of travel, inquire at the airline if the compartment is heated and pressurized. In some of the smaller planes this may not be the case, and they are unsuitable for shipping cats. Also, different lines have different safety provisions for shipping cats. Some will not accept live animals when the temperatures on the ground are below 45 degrees or above 65 degrees Fahrenheit. Some ask that you agree to pay the charges for the animal if no one is there to meet it and it has to be returned to you. These requirements are the result of new legislation to protect live animals in transit, and should be welcomed by every concerned cat owner. Unfortunately, there is still very little concern for the safety of your pet on flights, and what could be an excellent mode of transportation, is not. There are a few things, however, that you can do to improve the situation, some of them surprisingly simple.

Preparation starts with the travel container. You can buy travel carriers for small pets in every pet shop, varying in size, price and material, or you can buy one directly from the airline. Most airlines will supply you, at a very reasonable price, with a *Vari Kennel,* an excellent, sturdy container of high-impact, crush-proof plastic. It even dismantles to make a pet bed later on. To keep kitty warm and comfortable inside, fill it with shredded newspapers. Of course, your SnoWhite may emerge looking somewhat like a chimney sweep, but the black from the print will come off in the wash, and it is better to have a healthy but dirty cat than one with sniffles. In addition, newspapers are nice and crinkly, and cats love to bury into them. If the trip is a long one, line the bottom of the container with disposable diapers; they will help your kitty to stay relatively dry and comfortable. Including a litter pan is generally not advisable, since it takes up too much space, and is likely to get dumped out. If the carrier has no water dish in the door, tape a small bowl to the front. Then kitty can be offered a drink during stopovers. Food is generally not needed, since most cats will eat it all at once. Your cat is better off fasting for a day before a trip, settling its stomach, and averting airsickness. Although cats are supposed to be immune from motion sickness, I have cleaned up after many carsick ones.

Now that the inside of the carrier is ready for your little traveler, prepare the outside. This means that you must plaster the entire carrier with large signs proclaiming the destination of your cat. Don't rely on the tag the airline attaches—no one ever seems to read that. The only way to prevent your cat from going to Palm Beach, Florida, when you are sending him to Anchorage, Alaska, is to write this information on the container so many times that even the most nearsighted airline employee cannot miss it. If the airport to which your little cat is traveling is different from the town in which the person who picks him up lives, make sure to mention this on the label. For instance, you may write across the top: Cat to Missoula, Montana, and then follow with the address listing Kalispell, Montana. Too much bother? This is much less of a chore than waiting for your cat at ten o'clock at night only to be told that he did not arrive because (a) he was never loaded, (b) he was unloaded one stop too early, (c) he was unloaded two stops too late, (d) he is a figment of your imagination, and (e) he has turned into the Flying Dutchman!

Next comes a trip to your vet. Most airlines require a health certificate that is no more than one week old and states that your cat is free from communicable diseases and does not have rabies. In addition, in many states a rabies shot is required for shipping. Your vet should be able to tell you all this, and supply you with the necessary documents. Now call your airline to check if the flight is confirmed, and you are ready to take off. Be at the airline freight office an hour before departure, since there is still more paper work to be done. And don't forget to insure your cat for a whopping sum. Although this is only a theory among cat people, it seems that the airlines do show a little more respect and consideration for a cat that is insured for several hundred dollars. All of a sudden he becomes valuable cargo.

And now it is time to say goodbye to your cat. Are you worried that he may be terribly upset by the trip? Actually, most cats take their traveling in stride, and may spend their time in the air peacefully snoozing. Of course, you could have had him tranquilized, but tranquilizers are notably tricky, and what sends one cat off to dreamland, turns another into a raging tiger. Ask your vet at least a week in advance to prescribe some medication and try it out. Observe your cat and have the dosage adjusted, if necessary. But chances are that your traveling kitty will be a great deal more relaxed than you, and that he won't need any medication at all.

Car Travel

Air travel is generally for trips of long distance, and most cats will have their first journey in the family car. If you play your cards right, your kitty might even enjoy the adventure. But first he has to learn to get used to the motion, otherwise he will fly into a panic every time the wheels start turning. Therefore, he should take his first trips in a travel carrier. Let him start by getting used to this contraption. Even though most cats are inveterate closet dwellers at home, they will view anything that looks like a trap with deep distrust. And if the carrier means only a trip to the vet for your house tiger, he is sure to disappear every time the nasty thing is taken out. To prevent such suspicions, leave the carrier around, and invite kitty to investigate. Being a compulsive snooper, he won't be able to resist this invitation, and soon he will be happily crawling in and out of his new "toy."

Susie is at home on, in, and around the car. Most cats quickly adjust to car travel and may even enjoy it. *Urcia*

The safest way for cats to travel, whether by air or car, is in a sturdy, roomy travel carrier. Such carriers are available at pet shops or from the airlines. *Urcia*

Once he is familiar with the carrier, he is ready to travel. Try a short drive for a starter, and don't be dismayed if your cat chooses to howl all the way. The motion is strange to him, and he is telling you so. After a while, he will get used to it, but you will notice that the protests are likely to start up again every time you change speed or altitude. He doesn't like it when his ears pop when going up or down hills. If your cat is still a kitten, he may also enjoy sharing his carrier with another small cat. Two seem to feel more secure than a solitary one. After a few practice trips, most cats and kittens have adjusted and are comfortable enough to sleep the hours away.

If your little tiger is a calm, stable type who is not easily upset by strange sights and noises, you may decide that now is the time to let him out of his box so that he, too, can watch the world go by. But do this only when you share the car with another person, and never when you are driving alone. Someone may be needed to quickly return kitty to his box if the necessity arises, such as having to roll the window down to pay a toll at the booth. If your car has a shelf under the back window, place a blanket or cat bed there. Most cats like to look out while comfortably stretched out, and a view in the back is much less alarming than in the front. It may also be a good idea to let him wear a harness and leash. Cats are very quick and he may slip out the car door before you even notice him. In such a case it is much easier to grab a leash than a slippery cat.

For longer trips, place a litter pan on the back floor. If your kitty rides in a carrier, you can take a rest stop and let him out to use the pan. If he travels free on the seat, he will have easy access at any time.

Staying at Motels

Traveling, whether by air or car, sometimes means staying at a motel. Here the cat owner has an advantage over the person who travels with a dog. Motel owners are often rather narrow-minded, and if you drive up to the office with your large, friendly Saint Bernard drooling out of the back window, there may be very little welcome awaiting you. But a kitten in a traveling box is a much more harmless and—let's admit it—much less visible pet. However, cats aren't always welcome either, and the motel may sport a large sign saying: No Pets Allowed. Do you know who put it there in many cases? Your fellow cat owner. He may be the one who dumped litter into the toilet and clogged up the plumbing for a week. His tom may have sprayed the sofa with indelible odor. His frisky kitten may have shredded the shower curtains. No wonder the place has become off limits for pets. The "ugly" cat owner spoils it for us all, so don't be one. Supervise your cat's activities at all times and lock him up in his carrier if you have to leave the room. As for that spraying tom, he should be left home in the first place.

Fortunately, there are many motels that welcome pets, maybe because, as one motel manager confided, they don't run off with the towels

Korats like Gr. Ch. Kon Lek Lek Narawn Charanya are known as cats with a passport since they have traveled all the way from Thailand. Breeder/owner: Col. Wm. O'Neill.

A Rex kitten inspects the view from his motel window. Well-mannered cats are accepted at many motels if their well-mannered owners make sure to leave the room clean and dispose of litter in the trash. *Manus*

or burn cigarette holes into the mattress. Such a motel or hotel will welcome your four-footed companions. See to it that it continues to do so. For a starter, you should ask for a room at ground level, if possible. Even if your kitten is quiet and well-mannered, his little feet running across the floor sound surprisingly like an elephant stampede to the person in the room below. On the ground floor he won't be upsetting other guests, and can be allowed to stretch after a long, cramped ride. To keep his litter from scattering all over the carpet, set up the pan in the bathroom, and dispose of the contents by wrapping it and throwing it into the nearest outside trash container. And for the sake of your cat, make sure that all windows are closed before you release him in the room. After all, you don't want him to lose you in a place full of strangers.

Traveling need not be an ordeal for cats or cat owners. After all, show cats do it all the time. And there are special treats in store for even the most home-loving cat. He is allowed to sleep with you, a privilege he may not have at home. There will be interesting new sights, such as watching the seagulls from an eighteenth story window (be sure it is closed!). He will receive lots of attention, and he will be with you most of the time. So the next time you wonder what to do with kitty during your vacation or business trip, why not take him with you? You may both enjoy the experience.

9

The Ego Trip

ALTHOUGH THEY ARE called cat shows, most of these competitive affairs are really people shows. Cats, if given a choice, would probably prefer to stay home, except for a few dedicated people-watchers who enjoy sitting in their snug cages and watching the world parade by. But for cat owners who have been bitten by the show bug, cat shows are a necessity. They will brave long drives in miserable winter weather, early hours when most people are still sleeping, and all this for a few moments of glory when a judge says: "This is my Best."

To the novice show exhibitor, the whole affair may appear complicated and confusing. He does not know what all the different ribbons are for that decorate the cages, he is worried about doing the right thing at the right time, and he is bewildered by the talk of the old-timers who casually refer to color wins, Grand Champions, and specialty judges. Fortunately, such a feeling of being lost does not last long. Soon our novice exhibitor will be able to compete with the old hands in show "knowhow," and will try to out-expert the experts.

Preparing to Participate

What does it take to participate in the strange world of cat shows? First of all, you need a cat. This may be a purebred Persian or Siamese with ten generations of Champions behind him, or a multi-colored mixed breed with a tail longer than his ancestry. For the former, there are champion shows, and for the latter, the competition is among household pets.

Let's look at the champion show first. Such a show is held by a cat club under the sponsorship of one of the nine registering associations in the United States. Each association has slightly different rules, and most

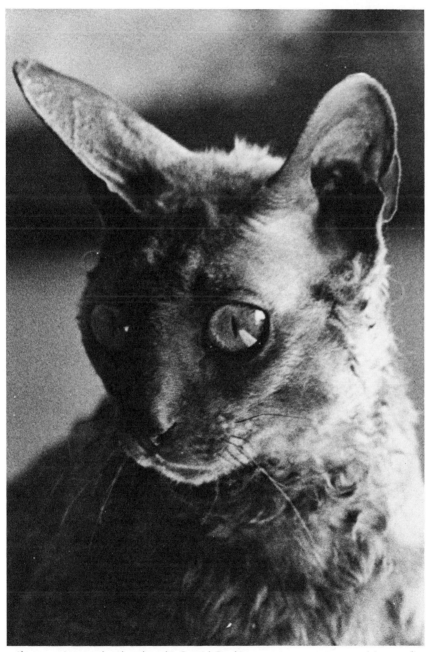

If your cat is a purebred, such as this Cornish Rex kitten, you may want to enter it in one of the many champion cat shows. *Oswald*

require that the cat to be shown is registered in the association books. This is no problem, since your purebred usually has papers from one or more associations. All you need is to find the right show, and he can be entered. However, there are age limits. Kittens must be at least four months old, and at eight months old they automatically become adults and can no longer compete in the kitten class. Young adults start out in novice or open classes, depending on the association. They then pass through a number of consecutive steps to reach the title of Champion. If they have shown exceptional quality, they may be able to fulfill the ultimate dream of every show participant and receive the coveted title of Grand Champion.

But wait, we are not that far along yet. Your purebred house tiger is still a beginner, and you have just decided to try your luck for the first time. How do you locate a show? Most of the major cat magazines publish a list of shows and locations every month, and you can easily find out when one is being held within a reasonable distance from your home. Write to the entry clerk, who is listed in the announcement as EC, and ask for some entry blanks. You will also notice some other mysterious abbreviations such as AB and SP, but we discuss those later. If you are not able to find a cat magazine, give the local cat club a call and ask about shows. Almost every larger city has such a club—or several—that will only be too happy to provide you with the information.

The entry blank is usually quite self explanatory, and asks for such items as the parents of your cat, his birthdate, registration number, and description. Fees for entry vary, with inflation having taken its toll in the past few years, but remember that your entry fee entitles you to show your cat to at least four judges, so it is really quite a bargain. There is usually a deadline for the entries, and it is a good idea to send yours in early since shows are restricted in the number of cats they can accept, usually 150–200 for a one-day show, and double that amount for a two-day extravaganza.

Bathing Your Cat

Soon your acceptance to the show will be mailed to you, and now it is time to get ready. Of course, we all know that your cat is Miss America, but she will be competing with 150 or 200 other Miss Americas, so some added touches are needed to bring out her perfection. As a starter, you may want to bathe her. Bathe a cat? Why certainly. Although Miss Shorthair Kitty does a very creditable job keeping herself neat (longhairs need your help since they don't have a built-in tangle remover), her fur can get greasy, dusty, and stained. Since most cats do not consider washing an experience that should be mentioned in polite company, you may want to get everything ready before you drag your cat out from under the sofa. You will need several large towels, a mild shampoo, vinegar diluted with water for a rinse, and if yours is a white cat, some laundry blueing to add to the bath water. Fill both halves of a divided kitchen sink with warm water, and add the vinegar mixture on one side. This will be your rinse water.

Now it is time to get kitty, and slowly lower all four feet into the water. Turn her face away from you, otherwise she will try to use you as a scaling post to get out of the bath. Gently and slowly start soaping her all over, especially under the armpits. Males should also get an extra scrubbing beneath the tail where a gland is located that secretes an oil that causes the so-called stud tail, a rather unsightly condition. Never wash or soap a cat's face. Next, lift her up and place her into the rinse water, and with a small cup start pouring the water over her back until all the soap has been washed out. By now, she may protest loudly, and will be very happy to be lifted out and wrapped in a large towel. Pat her as dry as possible, then get ready for the biggest chore—finishing the job with a hair dryer. Since dryers are noisy, most cats fear and hate these contraptions and suddenly seem to develop five or six extra feet just to get away from your grip. If your kitty has fairly short hair, you may decide at this point to spare her and yourself the ordeal and place her on a clean towel in a warm room. With her licking and shaking, she will soon be nice and dry. But your longhair must have help, and the dryer is an unavoidable necessity. You can save yourself some of the battle if you place your cat inside a travel carrier, and blow air through the window or door. Make sure that the temperature does not get too hot within the container. Finish the job with a brush and comb, and soon you will have an immaculate, sparkling cat who will head for the dustiest spot in the house as quickly as possible to remove any trace of her unwanted bath.

Chances are that after her bath your cat may resemble the girl who has just had a permanent and "can't do a thing" with her frizzy locks. When you washed out the dirt, you also removed quite a bit of the natural oil in the hair, which needs a few days to be restored. Therefore, plan ahead. Most long-haired cats, as well as slick-coated shorthairs such as the Siamese or curly-coated ones like the Rex, should be bathed about a week before the show. An exception are plush-coated cats like Russian Blues who are at their best when they are fluffed out; they can be bathed the day before the show. And of course, white cats may need some touchup or an entire bath shortly before their day of glory, since it is impossible to keep them immaculate over several days.

What Happens at a Cat Show

Your entry fee entitles your cat to a single cage, usually $21'' \times 21'' \times 21''$, which is furnished by the show management. A larger, double cage may be rented for an extra fee. In addition, you will find that litter is provided at the show, and in most cases food will also be supplied for your cat. The rest, however, is up to you. Since the wire cages allow views of the neighboring

Two Devon Rex kittens are almost obscured by
the many ribbons they have won at this show.
Chappell

Tortoiseshells are among the many colors
accepted for showing by cat associations.
Ellie Miller

A Siamese kitten is proud to have won Best
Kitten in Show.   *La Vond Thompson*

Colorful rosettes like these are awarded to the
top ten cats in each show ring.   *Urcia*

cats, you must curtain them off on three sides. This will prevent your cat from taking undue dislike to his fellow exhibit next door. The color, material, and arrangement of the curtains is left entirely to your imagination, but remember that a spraying tom—and he need not be your own—can turn the most spectacular drapes into a soggy, smelly mess in need of washing, so make sure your curtains can be laundered frequently. The wire cages have no floors, so you will also want to cover the bottom with a piece of rug to keep your cat comfortable. While there is no rule about covering the top, your cat will feel more secure in an enclosure that is protected on all sides. A small litter pan will complete the furniture for a well-equipped show cage, and it should be rather small unless you want your cat to spend the day sitting in it for want of a better spot. An aluminum cake pan is excellent for this purpose. Some exhibitors also like to provide their cats with a water dish, but the cat usually spills the water and gets himself wet. It is better to offer him a drink from time to time, but remove the dish when your cat shows no interest.

Cage Decorations

If this is your first cat show, you will probably take a good look around to see how the other exhibitors furnish their cages, and you may be in for a shock. Up to now you had considered your blue checkered curtains and your blue piece of carpet on the floor a very suitable environment for your cat, but your neighbor has surely outdone you by setting up a miniature western bar in his cage, complete with tiny glasses and red velvet bar stools. Don't feel too bad, he is simply competing in a contest for best decorated cage. Most shows have a theme, and offer a rosette or a small gift to the most imaginative and clever exhibitor who manages to decorate his cage according to the topic the club has chosen. If you have decorating skills, you too can compete, but if your talents do not lie in that direction, don't fret. Your set-up is quite adequate, and will not influence your cat's chances in the show ring. You will also discover that decorating a pretty cage is usually a game for pet owners who participate just for the fun; the true enthusiasts and breeders who attend many shows during the season seldom bother with those details.

Essential Equipment

More important is the equipment you will need during your day of showing. This includes, first of all, the necessary grooming paraphernalia. The owner of a longhaired cat will need one or more brushes, a so-called Belgian comb, powder, a tear stain remover, grooming chalk, and (unless he wants to look like an escapee from a flour mill) a grooming apron or lab coat to protect his clothing. The owner of a shorthair can get along with less, but will also need a brush, a chamois cloth to polish his cat (if he is of

93

the super shorthaired variety, such as a Siamese or Burmese), and some tissues to wipe away dirt from eye corners. It is a good idea to keep all this grooming equipment in a small suitcase ready for use at all times. Other items on the show exhibitor's list should include a can opener for cat food cans, a nail clipper for last minute trims, some cotton swabs to wipe out ears, a dish for food and one for water, and a few wire twists to anchor a cage door securely and prevent a possible escape artist from exploring the show hall on his own. Old hands at the show game also recommend taking along some extra food and litter just in case the show management is late in providing them, and a hair dryer for a cat who needs a last minute emergency bath. Owners of white cats are particularly urged to be prepared. It is truly amazing how skilled a white cat can be in messing up his sparkling pure color by rubbing against greasy cage bars, or by proving that motel chambermaids don't always sweep out under the beds.

Health Precautions

All set and ready? Then the fun can begin. Read the show flyer to see if the show you are attenting is *vetted* or *unvetted*. The former term means that your cat has to pass a veterinary inspection at the door of the show hall, and such inspection is provided during a given time preceding the actual show. If the show is unvetted, you may go directly to your cage after picking up your entry numbers at the door. Since vetting is a somewhat lengthy procedure, more and more shows are dispensing with it, but show management still keeps a sharp eye out for any cat showing signs of ill health. Such an entry is barred from the show. Rules stipulate further that any kitten or cat from a house where there has been an infectious illness or fungus is barred from participating for 21 days. Nonetheless, where so many cats congregate there is always danger of infection, and any cat or kitten taking part in a cat show should have had all his vaccinations.

The Show Begins

It is now ten o'clock, the advertised starting hour, and you, the novice exhibitor, are anxiously awaiting the next events. Relax! Any cat breeder will tell you that few cat shows ever start on time. You may as well learn right now that much of your time at shows is spent waiting—waiting for the start, waiting for one's cat to be called up, waiting for the finals. The name of the game is waiting. Use the time to familiarize yourself with the location of the rings so that you know where to go when your cat is wanted in ring two or three. As the show hall gets more crowded with exhibitors and visitors, you may notice that your cat is very tense during the trip from cage to show ring. Be sure to carry him properly, or you may lose him. There is a way that will give you almost absolute control over his contortions and

Those who love the unusual will be fascinated by the variety of breeds at a show. This Devon Rex, Hassan Chutney, is very striking. *Chappell*

International Champion Katzenburg's Josie is an example of the many fine show cats that can be seen at a cat show. *Nagel*

keep you from getting scratched. With your right hand reach around his body and firmly grasp him in front of his chest. His body is now imprisoned between your side and your arm and he cannot wriggle free. If he tries to kick with his hind legs, all you need to do is move your elbow closer toward your body and he will be helpless. For added control, place your left hand across his neck right behind his head. You will notice that some exhibitors carry cats on their shoulders or across their outstretched hands. Remember, before you try this, that these cats are old pros, veterans of many shows who aren't surprised by anything. Is yours? If not, better hang on to him. Some toms get very upset at the sight of the other cats they pass on their way. Covering their eyes often helps to relax them.

Now, take a look at the catalogue that you were handed at the door. It lists all entries by breeds, first the longhair kittens, then the shorthair kittens, the longhair adults alphabetically by breed, the shorthair cats the same way, and finally the alters, again divided into longhair and shorthair breeds. Find your entry and make sure that his name, parents, birthdate, owner, and class are listed correctly. If not, find the master clerk and tell him or her of any necessary corrections. Cats that are listed wrong will lose all their wins, so it pays to be careful.

Judging

Finally, about half an hour late, the loudspeaker crackles to life and the announcer welcomes everyone to the show. He reads a list of absentee entries, then announces that ring one is now ready for kittens 23 to 30. Soon the other rings come to life, too. Ring clerks place numbers above the cages behind the judges' tables, and exhibitors put cats into these cages. Your cat has a number, too, and it will be called as soon as your breed is judged. A judging schedule at the back of the catalogue will inform you of the order in which each ring will call the different breeds. As soon as your entry number is announced, take your cat to the ring, check him once more (ears clean? eyes bright?), put him into the cage, and then take a seat up front. Your ordeal is about to begin. The judge, who has been careful not to pay any attention to the cats as they are being placed in the cages, now consults his book. The breed, number, and class of the entry are the only details he has. He does not—or should not—know whose cat he is evaluating. This is serious business. Exhibitors are not permitted to talk to the judge while he is officiating; any necessary comments have to be addressed to the clerk sitting beside the table and entering the wins in the catalogue.

Watching a skilled judge at work can be quite enjoyable. One by one he takes the cats out of their cages, places them on his table, and, with deft movement designed to keep them off balance, he looks them over from all angles. Some cats are real hams; they pose for the judge and are not opposed to all this attention. Others are shy, and occasionally a reluctant beauty voices strong objections to this sort of treatment. In such a case the owner may be called in to lend a hand, and if the cat makes it clear that this nonsense better stop or else, he may be passed over for his more tractable colleagues. An experienced judge is also something of a showman, and often illustrates the finer points of the breed to the audience by bringing out the typical breed characteristics in each exhibit. Siamese—long and slender—are stretched out to full length; Persians are squarely dropped onto the table to display the full glory of their flowing coat.

As soon as all entries of a class are judged, the judge will start to hang ribbons on the cages. Newcomers to the show scene are always amazed at the amount and variety of ribbons some cats receive. Actually, there is method to this madness. First of all, each specimen is judged on his own merit, and then is compared with other present members of his class. This means that a male novice seal point Siamese is judged against all other seal point male novices. The best receives a blue ribbon, the second best a red, the third a yellow, and if there are more, they are out of luck. The blue ribbon winner also receives a red, white, and blue ribbon that establishes him as class winner. A given number of these class ribbons will eventually qualify him for the title Champion. In the meantime, the female seal point novices have not been competing with the males. They are in a class of their own, which will be judged in the same manner after the males. Following the novices, the Champions are judged, again males and females separately, and finally the Grand Champions. The latter do not receive any red, white, and blue ribbons, as these are no longer needed. After all classes are judged, the judge returns once again. This is the moment of decision, for now all the cats of the breed are competing for Best and Second Best of Breed. This honor can be awarded to any of the class winners, and, in fact, the judge may decide that the Second Best Novice is superior to all the other Champions and Grand Champions and award him the Second Best of Breed. This moment of truth being over, the exhibitors are told to take their entries back, and another breed will be called up.

Kittens and Alter classes are usually smaller and may only contain one member of a given breed, who then receives a blue ribbon unless the judge decides that the cat isn't good enough for such an award. Also, kittens, who do not compete for Championships, do not receive red, white, and blue class ribbons. Instead the judge, after having looked them over, picks his top five shorthair and longhair kittens (which means he is a Specialty Judge—SP), or his top five from both the shorthairs and longhairs combined (which means he is an Allbreed Judge—AB). Alters receive class ribbons and compete for Championships, but they are also awarded top-five winners at the end of their judging. For many years, Alter classes seemed to contain cats who were not quite up to the beauty standards of their whole colleagues. In the last few years, however, the quality of Alter exhibits has increased tremendously. This is a result of owners who enjoy showing their cats but do not wish to bother with breeding. They purchase an outstanding show animal for the main purpose of neutering and then showing him.

Grand Champions are the aristocrats of the cat shows. In order to achieve such a title, a cat has to fulfill additional rigorous requirements such as defeating 200 Champions or winning an award among the top five cats of the show. It takes an outstanding animal, time, and patience to achieve such distinction. And all the time, new hopefuls are treading hard on his heels. Cat showing is indeed a competitive activity.

The Awards

But what, you ask, are the rosettes in rainbow colors that hang on the wall behind the judges' tables for? Wait until the end of the show and you will see. After all the judging has been completed, numbers go up in the rings once more. These are the chosen, the top contenders in the show. Once more the exhibitors crowd around the ring while the judge announces his choices: his top class winners, such as Best Novice, Best Champion, or Best Grand; and his top five or ten cats, culminating in his Best in Show. (The actual lineup varies somewhat with each individual association.) This is the moment of glory each exhibitor dreams of. For this he has tolerated drafty halls, slick roads, and soggy hamburgers. And while his prize-winning Best Cat looks with boredom at his colorful rosette, the tearful owner thanks the judge, but already has his eyes on the next ring where the numbers are placed. Since each judge acts completely independently from the others, it is possible for a cat to be chosen Best more than once, but it is equally possible that the winner in one ring may not even figure in the final lineup of the next.

But what if your domestic tiger has no claim to noble lineage or breed, being one of the many colorful house pets of humble origin and mysterious parentage? He, too, can have his day in the sun (or rather, his proud owner can). Household pet shows are often held in conjunction with championship show, or they may be put on separately by a local cat club. The basic routine is the same, but the criteria are less clear cut. The judges look mostly for a well cared for, handsome animal that represents all the best qualities of the feline. As such, he will gather his ribbons and will be awarded a colorful rosette, perhaps even the famous Morris Trophy, which is never given to a purebred but always to the most outstanding household cat in a show. In recent years, the owners of pet cats have decided that they, too, want more glory for their cats, and some have joined registries that give their alley tom a name and a number on an official-looking document. But it is certain that yellow Morris or brown tabby Susie couldn't care less. Unlike his silly human, a cat needs no piece of paper to know that he is truly somebody.

Hu-Man's Sakura-Ko of Chipmunk is one of the few cats to have achieved the coveted title of Supreme Grand Champion. Bred by M. Whitehead, owned by Kay Hanvey.

Roger Michael

A little Russian Blue kitten poses with his awards. Kittens may be entered once they are four months old. *Rindfleisch*

This little fellow preferred to stay home and is just as happy as his show cousins.
Graham

And so another cat show comes to an end. It has been fun for the winners, and the losers always have the consolation of "next time." Cat lovers have gotten together to talk "cats," to share information, and to admire some of the most handsome felines in the country. There has been some keen competition, but most take their wins and losses with good grace. Why don't you give it a try and find out what this ego trip is all about? It's a great way to spend a weekend, and you may return with a new respect and appreciation for your family tiger. And that is what cat shows are really all about.

Part Two

The Breeds

Siamese (seal point). Gr. Ch. La Vond's Chai Luang. Breeder: La Vond Thompson. Owner:
Mary Elizabeth Sayles   *Jal Duncan*

Siamese (lilac point). Ch. Shensi Ismene. Breeder/owner: Mathilda Unruh. *Jal Duncan*

10

The Choice Is Yours

THERE ARE BASICALLY two kinds of cat lovers—shorthair fans and longhair fanatics. To those who prefer the sleek lines and simplicity of grooming that the shorthair presents, it is totally incomprehensible how anyone in his right mind would want to spend hours with brush, powder, and comb to restore his pet to its glory. The longhair owner, on the other hand, explains that he gets great satisfaction from having created a fluffy vision of loveliness, and sees little merit in the simple care of the shorthair. To argue the advantages of either type of cat is rather useless. After all, one of the attractions of the cat world is that it offers such a wide variety for every taste—from the fluffy to the hairless, from the curly to the slick, and all this in a veritable rainbow of colors. Let's meet them all.

Shorthairs

First and foremost, there is the *Siamese.* Siamese have been with us so long that they have become almost the embodiment of the purebred shorthair cat. The first recorded pair of Siamese was brought from Bangkok to England in 1884 by the British Consul General. Although some cat authorities have claimed that there were earlier Siamese in Europe, this has not been clearly established. The fact that these first cats came from Thailand also gave them their name, even though it is somewhat doubtful that the breed actually originated in Siam. Interestingly enough, in Thailand the Siamese is referred to as the Chinese cat, while the true native is the Korat, whom we shall meet a bit later. In 1890 the breed crossed the ocean from England to America, and soon Siamese began to appear in cat shows on both sides of the Atlantic. There are pictures of these early shows, where the cats were apparently not exhibited in cages but walked on leash just like dogs. Victorian catteries also sported maids in white aprons and caps who took care of the pampered pets, something that many a cat breeder of today might wishfully dream of. Incidentally, those early Siamese bore little resemblance to today's sleek, svelte creatures that compete at contemporary shows. They were apple-headed cats with round faces, sometimes crossed eyes, and the famous kink in the tail was not uncommon. After all, stories were told of a princess who had used her Siamese's tail to hang her rings during a bath, and how the cat had kindly crooked her tail to keep them from sliding off. Cat fanciers, even in those days, had vivid and charming imaginations. The earliest Siamese were all seal points, but were soon followed by the blue point (created probably through crossing in a blue shorthair), the chocolate point, and today's point colors ranging from red to tortie, bluecream, and tabby (lynx). Some associations feel that the latter colors do not represent the true Siamese and have them classified as *color points.*

The popularity of the Siamese spread very quickly, and today these cats comprise the biggest show entry among the shorthairs. In addition, there are legions of the so-called household Siamese, unregistered cousins who, from somewhere in the huge genetic pool that lies behind all American alley cats, have drawn the distinctive coloring of the light brown body and the dark feet, ears, and muzzle. These cats usually lack the creamy white or very light body of the show Siamese because in our colder climate the colors tend to darken. Even top show specimens have only a short time during which their color is truly outstanding. At an age when a Manx is just starting to come into his own, most Siamese are already too dark to compete and have to retire on their laurels.

The personality of the Siamese is famous. A talker and people lover, he does not like to be ignored or neglected and will tell you so at great length. Some people find the raucous voice objectionable, while others appreciate the intelligent interest this breed takes in everything. Siamese are quite adaptable to all forms of environment, city as well as country, and the sight of a Siamese frisking along on a leash is quite common. Their quick intelligence enables them to learn all sorts of tricks.

Among cat breeds, Siamese seem to have cornered the market for longevity. Many have reached the ripe old age of twenty years, and older ones are not uncommon. Despite their delicate, graceful appearance they are hardy cats, and somewhere in the background of almost every modern cat breed there are Siamese that have helped it to get established.

If you love a lively conversationalist who obviously enjoys your company, the Siamese is your cat.

Close to the Siamese is his cousin, the *Burmese,* but this relationship is not at all obvious when we see the two side by side. A compact, solid cat with a round head and a short muzzle, the Burmese resembles much more

Burmese. Gr. Ch. Ming-Ki Hot Chocolate. Breeder/owner: Wayne and Adrienne Tuman.
Jal Duncan

the domestic than the foreign shorthair type. Yet all Burmese in this country can trace their ancestry back to the mating of a Burmese, Wong Mau, with a Siamese male. Wong Mau arrived in the United Sttes in 1930 and was eventually given to Dr. Joseph C. Thompson, who set up a breeding program to perpetuate the sable brown cat. Since there was no stud available, a Siamese was called in, and soon the familiar medium-sized cat with the compact body, round head, boxy muzzle, deep golden eyes, and the short, close-lying coat was firmly established.

In Europe and Great Britain the Burmese had a slightly different development, and as a result resembles the Siamese much more closely, being longer and more slender. In addition, color breedings have developed Burmese in all colors of the cat world, including tortoiseshell and bluecream. These colors are not recognized in the United States, where most breeders have preferred the sable, although the champagne and the blue Burmese are recognized in some associations.

Less vocal than the Siamese, the Burmese is a very sweet tempered, affectionate cat. I have seen grown males drape themselves lovingly around their owner's neck, purring their hearts out,

There have been some problems for Burmese breeders in trying to create enough outcross lines, since basically every Burmese in this country is a close relative of every other. Since the British Burmese differ so widely in type, they are not used for outcrossing, and careful selection to avoid close inbreeding is required. This has made the Burmese a highly prized cat. If you are able to acquire one as a pet, you will have a companion full of both beauty and love.

Every breed has its legends, and *Manx* have many, mostly dealing with the reasons for their taillessness. According to one story, Noah was just about to close the door to the ark when the cat, tardy as usual, came running up and entered with one giant leap. But the closing door caught his tail and cut it off, and as punishment for this delay all Manx are a bit short in the tail department. Another story tells about the Manx Men on the Isle of Man who in the barbaric past practiced the custom of decorating their war standards with cat tails. Wise mother cats, to stop this practice, bit off the tails of their kittens at birth and thus created a tailless breed. More historically believable stories claim that the Manx arrived at their island several hundred years ago on board Spanish ships. Whatever their true origin, Manx are the symbol of the Isle of Man and even decorate a coin. During recent years, Manx have become rather scarce on their home isle, and the government now maintains a cattery to perpetuate the native breed.

Actually, Manx need not be tailless at all. In every litter of purebred Manx there can be kittens with fully developed tails (longies), with short stubby tails (stumpies), and with no tails at all (rumpies). The latter are the

Manx (bi-color). Quad. Gr. Ch. Cleomar Tinker Belle. Breeder/owner: L. Alice Hanbey.

Jal Duncan

true show cats, and instead of a tail they have a little indentation on their rear, lacking the last vertebra. It would be easy enough to breed rumpies by selecting only parents without tails, but nature has put a stop to this by slipping in a lethal gene. Rumpies bred to rumpies only will produce weak kittens, and in the next generation dead ones. So the stumpies as well as the longies are used for breeding purposes.

The Manx is also known as the bunny cat, since his hind legs are longer than his front legs. This, with the additional taillessness, gives him his characteristic hopping gait. Everything about this cat is round, from the rump (which is supposed to be like an orange) to the round face, head, and cheeks. The thick, double coat is accepted in all colors except Siamese derivatives. A true show Manx is usually expensive since breeding is costly and not easy, and produces unshowable kittens with tails as well as those without. However, if you are willing to overlook a little stump, you will be able to find many fine pet Manx.

A tough looking customer, the true Manx has a heart of butter. He is loving, even a little shy. He is also a hardy, self-sufficient cat who is an excellent mouser. If you have a Manx, you have a cat for all seasons.

The *Russian Blue* has sometimes been called the king of the shorthairs, and there is no doubt that he possesses a sort of regal presence. Like many older, established breeds the Russian Blue's origin is wrapped in mystery. He may have truly come from Russia, as his older name—Archangel Cat—indicates, because he as the plush double coat of most northern animals and does not mind cool weather. One of the first Russian Blues to arrive in England was actually imported from the city of Archangelsk in Russia, but the breed was also known as the Maltese. Most of today's Russian Blues are descended from British and Scandinavian imports, although legend has it that the Czar owned a Russian Blue, and well he may have, since this is a cat of distinction.

His heavy coat makes him appear larger than he is, as the true Russian Blue is a rather fine-boned animal whose every movement is surrounded by a silvery shimmer, caused by the silver tipping of each hair. Add to this bright green eyes and you have a strikingly beautiful cat.

Always among the rarer breeds, the Russian Blue nevertheless has been around a long time, and has enjoyed quite a bit of popularity. This is due to his appearance as well as to his impeccable manners as a pet. He is quiet, clean, and affectionate. One outstanding trait is his extreme loyalty to his owner and family, which has to be experienced to be believed. Strangers are treated with caution, and he prefers to observe them at first from a safe hiding place. If he does not approve, they will not even get a chance to see him. To those he loves he is willing to play the clown, and will even teach himself tricks for their amusement. Some Russian Blues are enthusiastic retrievers and will untiringly bring back a small ball or toy.

Some people believe that the Russian Blue is voiceless, but this is not true. Most of his conversation consists of a soft chirp, and he rarely ever raises his voice. Even females in season are less noisy and raucous than their counterparts in other breeds.

If you want a cat with class, with the manners of a queen and the innocent sweetness of a small child, choose a Russian Blue.

And then there is the *American Shorthair,* the true native. People often react with surprise when they learn that this cat belongs to a registered breed. After all, he is everybody's cat, the hard worker in the barn as well as the pussycat asleep on the porch swing. But he, too, has stories about his origin, and as a true American he traces it back to the Mayflower along with Miles Standish and John Alden. In fact, the early colonists prized their cats highly since they were useful in controlling the rodent population and saving the precious harvest. We don't know this for sure, but quite possibly an ancestor of today's shorthair was happily gnawing on a turkey wing during that famous first Thanksgiving.

The American Shorthair has his show career and appears in the ring in many colors. Especially popular is the flashy silver tabby—black stripes on a light grey background. A solid, no nonsense, compact cat, he has never lost sight of his original purpose as hunter and protector of the home; even the show standard demands a muscular, natural cat. And there are still some rags-to-riches success stories associated with this breed, since at least one association has an open registry and admits American Shorthairs of unknown parentage as long as they fit the standard.

If you acquire him as a show cat, he will come from carefully selected lines with close attention to color, pattern, and type, with a round head and a friendly expression. But he may also arrive at your door as a stray, willing to share love and affection for a square meal and a real home. If you offer these, he will repay you a hundredfold as a companion, hard worker, and friend. He couldn't care less whether his pedigree is ten generations long or as short as his tail, because he knows his real worth.

Fanciers of the *Abyssinian* claim that he is descended from the deified cats of ancient Egypt, and there is a certain resemblance between this intelligent breed, with its alert expression and large ears, and some of the Egyptian statues of god cats and cat gods. But this is a possibility that the Aby must share with the Egyptian Mau, and recent discoveries of mummified curly cats have also given the Rex a claim to such distinction. What is truly unique about the Abyssinian is his *agouti* color. This means that every hair of his short coat is ticked, that is, banded in black and various shades of darker brown. The red Aby, a newer development, is a genetically interesting variation since this red has unique characteristics and is not merely a color variation. The ruddy Abyssinian is more common, but both colors can appear in the same litter.

His color and appearance are strongly suggestive of the cougar, and there is a quality of wildness about the Aby that is not, however, part of his

Russian Blue. Ch. Katzenburg's Murka. Breeder/owner: Ingeborg Urcia. *Roger Michael*

American Shorthair (silver classic tabby). Ch. Sailway Guiseppe. Breeder/owner: Fay McDowell.

112

Abyssinian (ruddy). Gr. Ch. Udjat's Henre. Breeder/owner: Bob and Patti Taylor.

Jim Story

Cornish Rex (red mc tabby). Gr. Ch. Katzenburg's Amenhotep. Breeder/owner: Ingeborg Urcia.

Urcia

113

Devon Rex (tortoiseshell). Yclept Beth of Cantaur. Breeder: F. E. Chappell. Owner: Von and Tonya Fellner. *Chappell*

This Cornish
rex kitten,
Katzenburg's
Abigail,
is a happy
family cat.
Myers

character. The Abyssinian is a very friendly, companionable cat who will share everything, even your shower, since some members of the breed are rather uncharacteristically fond of water. His family life also resembles that of his large, wild cousins, since Abys are clannish and live in prides with the male quite willing to do his share in the raising of kittens. Other breeds are not always willing to accept the Aby, and he prefers his own kind anyway. Some cat breeders claim this is because an Aby smells different from other cats.

If an Aby shares your home, you will have a doer rather than a talker. He will want to share your life, lend a paw in the upbringing of his lively, often mischievous brood, and be happy to teach them all he knows— especially how to wrap his owner around his paw. As a show cat, he is a cat of moderation, neither extremely fine boned nor cobby, a truly balanced cat.

The six breeds just described are the old aristocrats of the shorthairs. They have been around a long time, have proven themselves both in the show ring and at the home scene. Recent years have brought a number of newcomers who also deserve your consideration. They are rapidly gaining popularity, even though they are still classed among the rarer breeds, and are not as frequently seen.

Among these newer shorthair breeds, the *Rex* may soon take first place in popularity. Yet the history of this interesting cat spans only 30 years. In 1950, a lady in Cornwall, England, discovered a funny little kitten in a litter of ordinary house cats. The small fellow had large ears, a long body, and most astonishing of all, a curly coat. It is history now that this strange little fellow was Kallibunker, the first *Cornish Rex* and ancestor of a new breed. His owner learned that he was a mutation, and with the help of a geneticist, a new breed of cat was born. Ten years later, in Devonshire, another cat lover discovered a kitten with unusual appearance and a little pixie face. He, too, became the ancestor of a new breed started through a mutation, this time known as the *Devon Rex*. Although both are curly cats, they have developed from different genetic mutations, and are separate breeds. The Devon's coat, body, and head are different than the Cornish's, and in the United States he is not quite as common as his Cornish cousin.

If you have never seen one of these unusual little cats your first reaction to the Rex may well be: Here is a cat that has been bathed but not dried. With his tightly marcelled coat, the Rex does indeed look like the product of a beauty salon. But like everything else about this cat, his hairdo is true and honest; he was born with it. Most cats have three types of hair in their coats: the guard hair, which is coarse and long and forms the outer layer; the awn hair; and the silky down hair. The Rex has only the down hair, which is incredibly soft to the touch. The coarser awn and guard hairs are absent.

In overall appearance, the Rex is also different from most other felines. He has huge ears, a long, slender body on high legs, and a thin, whiplike tail that seems to almost lead a life of its own. Combined, these add up to a very graceful animal who resembles those statues of ancient Egypt. But although the Rex may look skinny and fragile, there are muscles of steel under those velvety curls. He is a strong, agile cat, true to his domestic forebears.

And what is it like to live with a Rex? Picture a cat of high intelligence and vivid imagination, who simply adores people, and who finds life very interesting. He may cuddle up tightly right under your chin, he may perform graceful pirouettes for you with a piece of string, or he may spend a thoughtful ten minutes watching the water drain out of the sink and wondering where it went. Life is never boring with a Rex.

Man has created a number of appealing breeds and colors, but it is doubtful that he would have ever come up with anything as unique as the Rex on his own. And the same may be true for the *Scottish Fold,* another natural mutation. Here we have the sweet face of the domestic shorthair; a short, cobby body; round, kittenish eyes; and topping it all, the funniest little folded ears. It has been said that this cat appeals to the teddy bear complex in some people, and there is something in these round-faced, funny little cats that makes one want to cuddle them.

Scottish Folds originated in Great Britain, where they are no longer recognized by the Governing Council of the Cat Fancy. This was due to some breeding and genetic problems. They have increased quite a bit in number in this country, but there is a lethal gene in this breed, just like in the Manx, and raising them is not easy.

A few cat breeds have exotic names, even though their origin is close to home. Neither the Balinese nor the Himalayan, neither the Bombay nor the Birman have ever seen those exotic lands, but the *Japanese Bobtail* really originated in Japan, where he has been considered a good luck cat for hundreds of years. This long-legged cat with the unique little bunny tail is portrayed on century-old Japanese paintings, and a very colorful statue of a Bobtail, his paw raised in greeting, can be seen as a symbol of good luck all over Japan.

Of course, if you really desire all the good luck such a kitten can bestow, you must get a *mi-ke,* a tri-colored cat in black, red, and white. These were once most highly prized, and are still the traditional colors of the Japanese Bobtail, although other colors are bred and shown.

The little bunny tail, the most original thing about this breed, is not a stump like that found on some Manx. Instead, the pompom is formed by several tight kinks in the tail structure from which the hairs fan out.

Having been known as a bringer of good fortune must have built up the ego of this little cat considerably, because the Japanese Bobtail is a very friendly, self-assured fellow who likes to talk, and will answer you in a firm

116

Scottish Fold (silver tabby). Ch. Scotsie's Little Bit. Breeder/owner: Sue Pursinger.

Fudge

Japanese Bobtail (brown tabby and white). Gr. Premier Ogoniak Dima Dushenko. International Alter of the Year–TICA 1980. Breeder: Connie L. Voeth. Owner: Annouchka Anderson.   *Jal Duncan*

but soft voice. Perhaps he is calling down on you all the powers of good fortune!

The *Korat* is another cat with a passport. In fact, every Korat in the United States must show proof of his descent from Thailand in order to be recognized as a representative of his breed. Korats are also known as good luck cats, a trait they seem to share with most oriental breeds. Apparently, while Europe was busy burning witches and cats, more enlightened civilizations appreciated the little mouse catchers.

The biggest problem in owning a Korat is that people will always confuse him with other blue breeds. Yet the Korat does not sport the double coat of the Russian Blue, and his face is heartshaped and pointed, giving him a unique appearance.

Korat lovers claim that he is the true "Siamese," the real cat from Thailand. He is also known as Si-Sawat after a wild fruit with blue-grey seeds. He claims considerable antiquity and is mentioned in ancient documents going back as far as the fourteenth century.

In personality, the Korat seems to favor his Siamese cousin with a rather insistent voice. He is a rare cat even in his native country, but if you see a pair of huge, luminous, green eyes inspecting you solemnly at a cat show, stop a while and get acquainted with this unusual, poetic cat.

The *Egyptian Mau* is one of the few spotted domestic cats, and as the name implies, has actually been imported from the Near East. A long-time cat lover, Princess Natalia Troubetskoy of Russia was living in exile in Rome when she came into possession of a pair of imported spotted cats through her friendship with the Lebanese ambassador. In the 1950s she came to America and brought her cats with her. They became the foundation for most of the Mau in America.

In England, the Egyptian Mau is a man-made breed, and has little in common with the American variety.

Breeders of the Egyptian Mau point out that similar spotted cats can be seen on ancient Egyptian frescoes where they often function as trained hunters. Cats closely resembling the Mau can still be seen roaming the city streets and ancient ruins of Northern Africa and the Middle East.

The Egyptians come in three colors: silver, bronze, and smoke. The tail and legs have the typical tabby pattern. There is an "M" on the forehead, and the body is randomly spotted. They are medium-sized, medium-type cats with strong, muscular bodies.

Living with an Egyptian Mau offers the appeal of life with a wildcat, and all the conveniences of a domestic breed. The Mau is quiet, affectionate, and clean, gentle with those he knows, but a bit shy with strangers.

If you have a taste for the exotic, you will enjoy an Egyptian Mau, but you may have to search for one since the breed is still very rare.

The idea of trying to invent a better mousetrap is unusually apt when it comes to man-made cat breeds. With all the variety the natural breeds offer, there are still people who try to improve on what nature has created. For instance, wouldn't it be nice to have a cat that looks like a Persian but without the fuss and bother of keeping the long hair neatly groomed? The answer is the *Exotic Shorthair*. A cross between a shorthair and a Persian, the Exotic is similar to the Persian in body, but has a medium-long, very soft, very dense coat.

In temperament he displays the quiet dignity of his longhair ancestor, but from his shorthair parent he has inherited the ease of care. What more could one wish for in a pet?

The *Havana Brown,* contrary to his name, does not come to us as a refugee from Cuba, but is man's attempt to develop a solid brown cat with a warm, mahogany shade. In 1894 such a cat was shown in a British cat show under the name of the Swiss Mountain Cat, and solid brown cats have appeared naturally from time to time, although they are rare. These cats, however, were not breeding true due to their mixed ancestry. But to the true cat fancier, such obstacles are there to be overcome. Using Siamese and Russian Blues, tenacious breeders managed to develop cats in the color of a fine Havana cigar, and a new breed was born. To add to the overall color picture, the Havana has green eyes, a pink nose, and brown whiskers.

In personality, the Havana seems to have inherited much of the sweetness of his ancestor, the Russian Blue, and like this ancestor, the Havana also has a fine, soft voice. From his Siamese ancestors he has gained great agility with his paws, and is skilled at picking up objects to examine them more closely.

The many shorthairs that have gone into his making also have bestowed on him a sturdy body, medium size, and a smooth coat. But the Havana Brown should never be confused with the darker tone of the sable Burmese. If color is your thing, get a Havana Brown.

And so the list goes on with new chapters being added continuously to the story of the shorthair breeds. Want a black cat with copper eyes? There is the *Bombay,* a cross between a Burmese and a black shorthair. Want a naked cat? There is the *Sphynx.* The *Chartreux,* a big, blue cat, speaks with a French accent, and the *British Shorthair* is a bit of Old England. The *Oriental Shorthair* proves that man wasn't satisfied with the unique coloring of the Siamese—he had to have a solid color Siamese. And next year, or ten years from now, there will be new varieties of shorthairs not even dreamed of today.

One such breed that is just beginning to make its way is the *Singapura,* sometimes called the world's smallest cat, and certainly one of tomorrow's breeds. True to its name, the Singapura has come to us from Singapore, but its origin cannot be found among the houses of the elegant and rich. During an extended stay, an American cat lover noticed among the many half-feral cats that inhabited the drains and alleys of Singapore a number that showed the same ticking as the Abyssinian, but on a pale background

Korat.
Ch. Chirawan
Anwandontri.
Breeder/owner:
Karen van Haagen.
Jim Story

British Shorthair (white). Supreme Gr. Ch. Top Fashion's The Crisco Kid. 11th Best Cat–TICA 1982. Breeder: Daniel and Patricia Gorman. Owner: Brenda and Bill Kinnunen.

Oriental Shorthair (white). Supreme Gr. Ch. Clarion Cara Mia of Chipmunk. Breeder: Margaret Smith. Owner: Kay L. Hanvey. 5th Best International Cat 1982. *Jal Duncan*

Singapura, one of the newest breeds. Breeder/owner: Tommy Meadows.

122

rather than on red or ruddy. A pair of these little cats with huge eyes and dainty bodies went back with her to the United States where they became the foundation of what the breeder hoped would be a new breed. At this time, the Singapura has been accepted by a few registering bodies but has a long way to go to achieve full recognition by the general cat fancy.

Longhairs

Compared to the variety of shorthair breeds, the longhairs are the conservatives of the cat world. Why keep looking for new shapes when you already have perfection? Instead, breeders have created a rainbow of pleasing colors to suit any taste or decor. This is the case with the *Persian*. In fact, most people think of the Persian as the only longhair cat, although some other very attractive longhair breeds also claim the spotlight. It is, however, true that 90% of all longhair cats exhibited are Persians.

Describing the Persian seems almost redundant. Who hasn't seen this epitome of luxury relaxing on a silken pillow, his flowing hair spread elegantly around. One can almost see the maid industriously brushing My Lady the Cat's perfect coat. Yes, every Persian should have a maid. The fine, dense coat requires a lot of daily grooming, powdering, and combing, but the end result is worth the effort. With his beautiful, glossy coat, compact body, flowing tail, round innocent eyes in a stubby, sweet face, the Persian is the aristocrat among the longhairs.

As with most old, established breeds, the Persian's ancestry and origin are a bit of a mystery. The breed is believed to have come from Asia, and some naturalists point to the Pallas Cat, a longhaired, wild cat of the steppes, as the forerunner of the Persian. There is an actual resemblance, but it is obvious that centuries of breeding have gone into the creation of today's Persian.

Every Persian seems to know he is beautiful and likes to pose in a proper setting. A quiet, stable cat, he may yet surprise you with an unexpected streak of mischief, and a Persian kitten stalking his litter mates is a very droll sight. But don't laugh too hard; like all cats the Persian has a pronounced sense of dignity and does not easily forgive a loss of face.

Color is the big game among Persians. Besides the traditional blacks, blues, and whites we find such interesting variations as the shell cameo (a delicate pink) or the shaded silver. Need a cat who will give your home prestige? A Persian will always add class and refinement.

Although almost as ancient as the Persian, the *Turkish Angora* seems to have lost his popularity during the earlier part of this century. This lovely breed almost died out, and for a long time the cat world claimed that there was no such a thing as an Angora, that he was merely something like a Persian. From this identity crisis he was rescued when breeders in the 1950s imported some Angoras from the Ankara Zoo, where they had been

Persian (tortoiseshell). Ch. Halloween's Fire Opal. Breeder/owner: Margit F. Courturier.

Jal Duncan

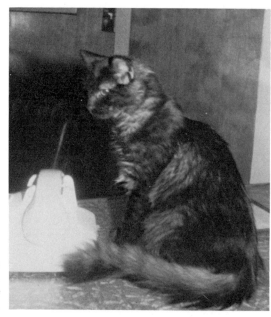

Turkish Angora (black smoke) kitten. Breeder/owner: Elaine Gesel.

preserved as a pure breed. This is also the region in Turkey where this cat seems to have first originated. According to legend, Kemal Attaturk, the famous Turkish leader and patriot, is supposed to return incarnated as an odd-eyed white Turkish Angora. This may be the reason why the Ankara Zoo only recognizes the white Angora, and until recently this was also the only acceptable color in the United States. But a few years ago, the colored Angora finally achieved his rightful place beside his white brother.

A proud cat with a lively manner, this cat is quite unlike the stockier Persian. He is slender, fine boned, and small with flowing hair and fluffy ruff that lack a matting problem. A Turkish Angora almost always looks well groomed with very little effort. His fluffy tail raised proudly across his back, he dances along—agile, curious, and graceful.

Second only to the popularity of the Persian is another longhaired breed, the *Himalayan*. Notwithstanding his name, the Himy would probably be very surprised if you asked him about his mountainous home country, because his breed is British and American made and has never seen Asia. As the product of a concerted effort to breed the Siamese colors in a Persian-type cat, the Himy can be seen in all point colors of the Siamese. Other than his coloring, he is a true Persian in coat and appearance.

Among all the breeds in the United States, the Himalayan has had the distinction of being the fastest growing in popularity, probably because for the cat lover he combines two of the most distinctive breeds, the striking Siamese and the luxurious Persian. He is an affectionate cat and will actually wilt from lack of attention. He expects to set his own rules around the house, and woe to the owner who violates them. His Himy will punish him by ignoring him until proper apologies are tendered. Yet he is also quite happy to put himself out to amuse you, and few other breeds are as willing to learn tricks. He may even master such feats as jumping through a hoop or rolling over. For the best of two worlds, why not choose a Himalayan.

The *Maine Coon* is often described as the only native American longhaired cat, but his rugged New England ancestors must have originated somewhere else. One story has it that Queen Marie Antoinette, in anticipation of the French Revolution, shipped some of her household goods and treasures for safekeeping to the United States where they ended up in New England warehouses. Among her treasures were certainly some of her noble cats, who became early immigrants to the New World. Another charming legend, but no more improbable, is that the Maine Coon resulted from a cross between a cat and a raccoon. With Maine Coon lovers it is "the bigger the better," and they are looking for a strong, heavy-boned, big cat whose broad, furred paws act like snowshoes in the harsh New England winter. All colors are recognized, but Maine Coons seem to favor the various shades of the tabby in brown, blue, and silver.

Himalayan (seal point). Ch. Ming-Ki Spring Breeze. Breeder/owner: Wayne Tuman.
Jal Duncan

Maine Coon
(brown tabby).
Ch. Kiskata's
Kutiga.
Breeder/owner:
Jane Cargill
and
Terry Oliverio.
Jal Duncan

Birman (seal point). Gr. Ch. Chittagong Wells Fargo. Breeder/owner: Patricia Hopps.
Roger Michael

Somali (ruddy). Ch. Rainkey's Windwilly. Breeder: Sheila Bowers. Owner: Gery
Bergstrom. *Jim Story*

Some are born with more than their regular number of toes, but such polydactylism is not desirable.

If you want a Maine Coon as a pet you won't have an easy time finding one. Their major concentration is still New England, although Coon breeders live in such far apart places as Arizona and Illinois.

A beautiful, white cat named Sinh was the faithful companion of a Burmese priest, as the legend about the *Birman* tells us. One night the priest was attacked by raiders who killed him. His faithful cat placed herself on his body. Suddenly her white coat turned a golden shade, her eyes became blue, and her legs became a deep velvet brown except for the paws, which remained white as a sign of purity. Despite the picturesque legend, however, the Birman is mainly a French creation, although it almost disappeared during World War II.

A medium-length coat prevents matting, and an attractive color scheme adds to the appearance of this regal cat. The white mitts and socks are the most important features, however.

These cats are still rare, and you are fortunate indeed if you own such a cat, which was once supposed to guide the souls of the faithful to paradise.

The major longhaired breeds are joined over the years by new creations duplicating the shorthair varieties but with the longer, flowing, silky coat. The longhair Siamese (not a crossbreed but a mutation) is known as the *Balinese,* the *Cymric* is a longhaired Manx, and the *Somali* sports the Abyssinian colors and type with a long coat.

Short or long, large or small, there is a cat for everyone. The choice is yours.

FROM THE PUBLISHER

We hope you have enjoyed reading Ingeborg Urcia's *For the Love of Cats* as much as we have enjoyed publishing it. There's a special feeling about cats shared by their people and we do think this book has the feeling all cat fans know so well.

By owning this book you show that cats have a special place in your life and the well-being of your cat is really important to you. Accordingly, you should know about *Cat Owner's Home Veterinary Handbook,* by Delbert G. Carlson, DVM and James M. Giffin, MD. Acclaimed by cat authorities everywhere, this 392-page volume is the most complete, up-to-date reference on feline health and illness in print for the lay owner. It's well-written, attractive, easy to use and understand and is the prime reference on your cat's health from kittenhood to old age. You'll be able to spot problems early and be better able to communicate with your veterinarian. You'll also be able to help your cat at home when professional attention is not indicated. Many a wise cat owner keeps a copy of *Cat Owner's Home Veterinary Handbook* within easy reach. You should do the same. You'll find this book in better pet shops or book stores. Get your copy today.